Figurative Inquisitions

 FLASHPOINTS

The FlashPoints series is devoted to books that consider literature beyond strictly national and disciplinary frameworks, and that are distinguished both by their historical grounding and by their theoretical and conceptual strength. Our books engage theory without losing touch with history and work historically without falling into uncritical positivism. FlashPoints aims for a broad audience within the humanities and the social sciences concerned with moments of cultural emergence and transformation. In a Benjaminian mode, FlashPoints is interested in how literature contributes to forming new constellations of culture and history and in how such formations function critically and politically in the present. Series titles are available online at http://escholarship.org/uc/flashpoints.

SERIES EDITORS:

Ali Behdad (Comparative Literature and English, UCLA), Founding Editor; Judith Butler (Rhetoric and Comparative Literature, UC Berkeley), Founding Editor; Michelle Clayton (Hispanic Studies and Comparative Literature, Brown University); Edward Dimendberg (Film and Media Studies, Visual Studies, and European Languages and Studies, UC Irvine), Coordinator; Catherine Gallagher (English, UC Berkeley), Founding Editor; Nouri Gana (Comparative Literature & Near Eastern Languages and Cultures, UCLA); Jody Greene (Literature, UC Santa Cruz); Susan Gillman (Literature, UC Santa Cruz); Richard Terdiman (Literature, UC Santa Cruz)

Figurative Inquisitions

Conversion, Torture, and Truth in the
Luso-Hispanic Atlantic

Erin Graff Zivin

NORTHWESTERN UNIVERSITY PRESS | EVANSTON, ILLINOIS

Northwestern University Press
www.nupress.northwestern.edu

Digital Printing

Library of Congress Cataloging-in-Publication Data

Graff Zivin, Erin, author.
    Figurative inquisitions : conversion, torture, and truth in the Luso-Hispanic Atlantic
/ Erin Graff Zivin.
        pages cm. — (FlashPoints)
    Includes bibliographical references and index.
    ISBN 978-0-8101-2945-0 (pbk. : alk. paper)
    1. Latin American literature—History and criticism. 2. Portuguese literature—
History and criticism. 3. Torture in literature. 4. Inquisition in literature. 5. Torture in
motion pictures. 6. Inquisition in motion pictures. 7. Torture—Social aspects. I. Title.
II. Series: FlashPoints (Evanston, Ill.)
PQ7081.G684 2014
860.9358—dc23

                                                                            2013032441

For Miles and Elias

Contents

Acknowledgments

The experience of writing a second book is markedly different from that of writing a first book. If the first book has its roots in the dissertation, and therefore always feels as if it were being written "for" something or someone else, the second book emerges out of a strange freedom: one is writing, simply, because one must write. At the same time, this project is the fruit of provocative and inspiring conversations and exchanges with a great number of people and, in this sense, is very much written "for" these others: if not out of an institutional or professional obligation, then out of a genuine intellectual debt. These people—teachers and students, colleagues and interlocutors—populate each page of this book, beginning with my former professors who are now dear friends, Sylvia Molloy and Gabriela Basterra.

I had the good fortune to begin my academic career at one of the most stimulating places to research Latin American literary and cultural studies. At the University of Pittsburgh, I taught—and learned from—a wonderful group of graduate students in the Department of Hispanic Languages and Literatures. I want to thank the participants of the "Interrogative Signs" seminar in spring 2008 for debating some of the early ideas for this book. The Center for Latin American Studies and the University Research Council Small Grants Program at Pitt supported preliminary research on this book.

After four years of being part of a commuting family, I won the lottery and was offered a wonderful job close to relatives and dear friends in California. Joining the faculty at the University of Southern California has thus felt like a homecoming in many ways. I can say with confidence that I have the best colleagues around: in the Department of Spanish and Portuguese, Sherry Velasco and Roberto Ignacio Díaz have been incredible mentors and friends, and my newest colleagues—Julián Daniel Gutiérrez-Albilla, Sam Steinberg, and Natalia Pérez—make the future at once incalculable and promising. I am also fortunate to be part of the Department of Comparative Literature and the Doctoral Program in Comparative Studies in Literature and Culture with Peggy Kamuf, Panivong Norindr, and many others who are protagonists in USC's vibrant intellectual culture. I want to extend a special thanks to the graduate students who participated in the "Aesthetics of Torture" seminar in spring 2011.

My work would be impoverished without the brilliance of the following interlocutors and friends: Nathalie Bouzaglo, Patrick Dove, Jonathan Freedman, Michal Friedman, Kate Jenckes, David E. Johnson, Jeffrey Lesser, Brett Levinson, Jacques Lezra, Emily Maguire, Alberto Moreiras, Ronnie Perelis, Justin Read, and Mariano Siskind, all of whom have had an impact upon this book. Many thanks to Vivaldo Andrade dos Santos and Ana Lee for proofreading the Portuguese translations, Ryan Trombley for his meticulous editing, the anonymous readers at Northwestern University Press for their invaluable feedback on the manuscript, and Henry L. Carrigan for his enthusiastic support of this project. I am grateful to live just down the coast from Karina Miller and Jessica Pressman, with whom I read, write, revise, laugh, complain, and practice yoga on a weekly basis, and without whom I would be in complete intellectual exile here in beautiful, sunny Solana Beach.

A lot has happened since I began to write *Figurative Inquisitions*. Miles and Elias—to whom this book is dedicated—were born and learned to crawl, walk, talk, run, and dribble a soccer ball as I drafted chapters. Simon began to read with a hunger that I remember experiencing as a child, and would often read next to me as I wrote. My parents, as well as Salina Bastos and Haley Calabrese, have loved and helped to care for my three wonderful boys so that I could work. Finally, for nearly twenty years, Josh has been my partner in crime and my rock. I owe him everything.

Preface: Inquisitional Logic

The interrelated practices of interrogation, torture, and confession are global phenomena that, while they have existed for several millennia, have resurfaced in public debates since the early 2000s after accounts of human rights abuses in U.S. prisons and "black sites" abroad began to circulate and, in early 2009, after a newly elected President Obama issued a directive to close the Guantánamo Bay detention camp as one of his first orders of business (a promise that has yet to be fulfilled).[1] In the years following these events, there has been a proliferation of discussion about the use of torture that has remained restricted to three principal fields: the legal (is it allowed?), the pragmatic (does it work?), and the moral (is it right?). What has often remained left out of the conversation—which revolves around the ostensibly competing demands of national security and universal human rights—is the seemingly less immediate but vital question of what torture *does*. What happens within the scene of interrogation and torture? What kinds of subjects and truths are produced through the acts of questioning and confession? Why, indeed, do we torture?

This book dwells upon the relationship between scenes of interrogation and the identities and discourses that are fashioned within these scenes by turning to the early modern phenomena of the Inquisition and Jewish conversion (*marranismo*), not so much to suggest that they constitute a foundational example of interrogation or torture (which can be found in Greek antiquity and earlier), but rather because the act of questioning within the historical context of the Inquisition offers a formal structure that sheds crucial light on both prior and subsequent instances of this practice. *Figurative Inquisitions* argues that literature, or literary criticism, is well positioned to make a crucial contribution to current debates on torture. By situating nineteenth- and twentieth-century aesthetic representations of the Inquisition within a broader tradition of interrogation and confessional narratives, this study aims to underscore the fictional or narrative quality of interrogation, as well as to evaluate the ethical and political consequences of these explicitly creative acts.

At the same time, this book is not really—or not only—about torture, but about something broader, more widespread, more insidious. Or rather, it suggests that torture is *symptomatic* of a broader phenomenon that I will call "Inquisitional logic," a concept that I develop in the following chapters through a discussion of *marranismo*, allegory, and torture. Inquisitional logic is the necessary companion of Spanish imperial reason in the sense attributed to it by Alberto Moreiras, who has convincingly argued that "Spanish imperial reason was strongly, if certainly not exclusively, marked by the process that led to the establishment of the Inquisition, first, and by both the discursive and material relations that Spain developed with the natives of the New World" ("Spanish Nation Formation," 5). Inquisitional logic represents the violent face of the dominant concepts of modernity: identity as reflexivity or self-presence (and difference as its corresponding mirror image), sovereignty, and the idea of the political as the Schmittian divide between friend and enemy. It accounts for the link between Inquisition and colonialism, given the historically and geopolitically specific conditions of imperial expansion across the Atlantic.[2] Inquisitional logic, finally, grounds itself in the violent conversion of others (Jews and Muslims in the Iberian Peninsula and indigenous peoples in the Americas), in the representation of the Americas as a new and eminently "convertible" world, and in the subsequent "reconversion" of these subjects through interrogation and torture. Conversion, in this sense, stands as the organizing principle of both Inquisition and colonialism, the totalizing violence of which can be understood as a response to internal instability and heterogeneity. This is particularly true of Spanish and Portuguese colonial expansion, given that both empires struggled to eliminate Judaism and Islam through conversion and expulsion from the Iberian Peninsula, while conquering ethnic and religious difference through annihilation, enslavement, and conversion in the New World.[3] By examining aesthetic (theatrical,

cinematographic, and narrative) scenes of conversion and violent interrogation, I aim to unpack the motives, desires, and anxieties that fuel
Inquisitional logic and imperial expansion across the Atlantic, as well
as more "modern" inquisitions—military governments in Brazil, Argen-
tina, and Chile and on the Iberian Peninsula, de facto dictatorship in
PRI-dominated Mexico, and U.S. McCarthyism—during the latter half
of the twentieth century.

Figurative Inquisitions is also very much a post-9/11 book. A product of the period immediately following the attacks on the World Trade
Center and the Pentagon, and the (one might say, far more brutal) responses to these attacks, as well as the initially promising but ultimately
disappointing attempt by the Obama administration to shift direction
on policies governing war and torture, this book seeks to identify links
between classical torture, Inquisitional interrogation, and contemporary
forms of political violence on both sides of the Atlantic. By focusing on
aesthetic (often, allegorical) scenes of conversion and torture, this book
draws attention to the specters of history that continue to haunt us in
the present day. *Figurative Inquisitions* attempts, moreover, to imagine
a way of thinking that might offer alternatives to the status quo. In this
sense, the book asks questions that are at once aesthetic, political, and
ethical, exposing the limits of Inquisitional logic while taking caution to
avoid overly reductive characterizations of what might lie on the other
side.

Taking as its point of departure the discursive and material encounters between torture, conversion, and aesthetics in the introduction, the
book proceeds to deconstruct three variations of such practices. Chapter 1 dwells upon aporias of *marranismo*, in both its historical and
symbolic forms, by reading aesthetic representations of the marrano,
or crypto-Jew, as a subject that guards a secret par excellence, and that
stands as the alter ego of the modern, sovereign subject, as Argentine
philosopher Ricardo Forster has argued. I claim that the marrano is
an aporetic, or paradoxical, figure that serves as the condition of possibility of the modern subject while simultaneously signaling its limit.[4]
Engaging philosopher Jacques Derrida's idea of the secret as that which
exceeds the play of concealment and revelation, I focus on a tension in
the aesthetic works that codify the marrano between, on the one hand,
the thematization of the secret related to the notion of *alêtheia* or unburied truth, and the marrano secret as that which exceeds readability
or representability. Chapter 2 charts a genealogy of Inquisition allegories that confront the violent political present through the past as ruin

or specter, in dialogue with critic Walter Benjamin's work on *Trauerspiel* and Derrida's writing on haunting. Moving beyond an interpretive approach that would seek to uncover a hidden, or censored, "truth" beneath allegorical language, I perform an operation compatible with my reading of marrano secrets, exposing textual and visual instantiations of that which refuses representation, or that which renders impossible the idea of (allegorical) truth. The tension between hidden truth as positive essence and the secret as irreplaceable singularity in both marranismo and allegory paves the way for a consideration of aesthetic scenes of torture and interrogation in chapter 3. If torture pursues the secret of the other (here, the crypto-Jew), literary scenes of violent interrogation likewise oscillate between the reproduction of Inquisitional logic, according to which the truth of the crypto-Jew is either accessible or inaccessible, and a subversion or refusal of such logic. The final chapter takes a step back from the Inquisition narratives that serve as the principal corpus of this study to consider "other" inquisitions. Reading scenes of police questioning in Portuguese novelist Jose Saramago's *Ensaio sobre a lucidez,* chapter 4 returns to the present-day War on Terror, the age of "you're either with us or against us." This last chapter allows us to pose directly a question that haunts the whole book, that is, what we mean by "literature"—a concept with a tormented relation to the field of ethics as well as to the notion of truth, and to the practices historically mobilized for producing, describing, or disclosing it.

Figurative Inquisitions

Introduction: Conversion, Torture, and Truth

TORTURE AND TRUTH

[Torture . . .] any act by which severe pain or suffering,
whether physical or mental, is intentionally inflicted on a
person for such purposes as obtaining from that person or a
third person information or confession, punishing that person
for an act committed or suspected to have been committed, or intimidating or dehumanizing that person or other
persons.
—U.N. Convention Against Torture

Truth, *alêtheia*, comes from elsewhere, from another place,
from the place of the other.
—Page duBois

The purpose of [torture] is to force from one tongue, amid
its screams and its vomiting up of blood, the secret of
everything.
—Jean-Paul Sartre

The main rationale offered by those who defend the practice of torture
is that the use of physical and psychological abuse as part of the interrogation of prisoners guarantees the extraction of the truth—generally
understood to be the acquisition of information that promises to save

hundreds, thousands, or millions of innocent lives—and that violent interrogation should therefore be sanctioned by governments that claim to be democratic. In recent decades, this argument has taken as its primary justification the "ticking bomb scenario," a hypothetical event imagined by philosopher Michael Levin in the 1980s and rehearsed by countless others since then, including Senator Charles Schumer following the attacks of September 11, 2001.[1] Levin invites us to imagine a fictional scenario in which authorities have arrested an alleged terrorist who possesses valuable information: the secret hiding place of a bomb set to detonate on the symbolically overdetermined date of July 4. Levin challenges us to come up with a reason why torture should *not* be used in such a situation, and grounds his argument in the two thematic or conceptual areas within which torture has been both defended and attacked: the practical and the moral. The practical, according to Levin's example, is quite simple: it goes without saying that torture in every case produces the facts needed by the torturer. Here, the link between torture and truth (the origins of which I discuss below) is taken as a given.[2] While the moral question is more complex, Levin argues that anyone concerned with the ethicity of torture would do well to examine his or her own conscience, sustaining that it would be unethical to *refrain* from using torture if it were to save the lives of millions of Americans.

There are a number of reasons why Levin's argument lacks logical coherence, as moral philosopher Bob Brecher and political theorist Jacques Lezra have demonstrated. In their recent books on torture and terror, respectively, Brecher and Lezra deconstruct the false scenario upon which Levin bases his case, exposing the ticking bomb scenario as fantasy. A number of factors support their theses, but I would like to underscore two here: the decidedly literary or mythological quality of the event (the incident in question happens on the 4th of July; the day is described as "fated"), and the faulty logic upon which it rests (it is virtually impossible to prove the existence of an attack that does *not* come to fruition).

The notion that torture produces the truth, always and in every case, goes virtually unexamined by Levin, though he is certainly not the only person—on either side of the debate—to miss this crucial point. This is because, if we are to follow the scholarship of Page duBois, the practice of torture in Western culture is intimately tied, since its inception, to classical notions of truth: "That truth is unitary, that truth may finally be extracted by torture, is part of our legacy from the Greeks and, therefore, part of our idea of 'truth'" (duBois, *Torture and Truth*, 5).

DuBois argues that some of the earliest instances of torture (*basanos*) in Western civilization appear intrinsically linked to the formulation of the idea of truth (*a-lêtheia*). By tracing the etymology of the word *basanos*, which originally referred to a touchstone to test the purity of gold, and which evolved, in Athenian culture, to signify a test of loyalty and, finally, to the extraction of truth from the body of the slave using force, duBois demonstrates that our very notion of truth is inseparable from the Western practice of torture: "the logic of our philosophical tradition, of some of our inherited beliefs about truth, leads almost inevitably to conceiving of the body of the other as the site from which truth can be produced, and to using violence if necessary to extract that truth" (6).

The "truth" with which torture ostensibly concerns itself, however, remains vague and difficult to define. Those who defend the use of torture (recently this has come to be called "enhanced interrogation") cite as the goal of such a practice the acquisition of the truth understood as fact: specifically, the empirical facts of a given situation (such as the precise location of the hypothetical ticking bomb). In reality, however, instances in which torture has elicited useful information are few and far between, as Elaine Scarry argues in *The Body in Pain*: "for every instance in which someone with critical information is interrogated, there are hundreds interrogated who could know nothing of remote importance to the stability or self-image of the regime" (28). The collection of pieces of evidence or "truths" (with a lowercase "t"), according to Scarry, only masks the actual function of torture, which is the fabrication of the "Truth" (with a capital "T") of power. In this sense, the *content* of what is confessed—the cognitive or constative element of confession, rather than its performative quality—turns out to be largely irrelevant. Instead, it is the dehumanization and destruction of the voice, language, and world of the prisoner (and subsequent invention of the "truth" of the regime) that stand as the de facto goal of torture (Scarry, *The Body in Pain*, 35–36).

Within ancient Greek legal culture, torture was performed upon the body of the slave in order to extract the truth of the free man: often, the slave was summoned to provide incriminating evidence about his own master. It is crucial to understand this practice within the broader social and political context of classical Athens, "a world turning upside down" (duBois, *Torture and Truth*, 10). During this period of identitary instability, it was imperative to establish a division between citizen and noncitizen (a relatively straightforward task) and slave and free man (a more difficult undertaking, given that a born slave could be set free and a free man could be enslaved, subverting the notion that one is "essentially" one or the other). Torture in Athenian law therefore "forms part of an attempt to manage the opposition between slave and free, and it betrays both need and anxiety: need to have a clear boundary between servile and free, anxiety about the impossibility of maintaining this difference" (duBois, 41). DuBois's argument underscores the relationship between competing notions of "truth" at work in the historical practice of torture: if on the surface, torture aims to uncover facts about a legal crime, what torturers *really* seek to create (and turn into "truth") is the difference between same and other. As Scarry explains, the radically corporal, tangible quality of pain confers upon the scene of torture an element of truth, so that the ambiguity of the division between slave and free man can be inscribed—quite literally—upon the body of the other.

Each of the "meanings" of *basanos* (a touchstone to determine the purity of gold, a test of loyalty and, finally, the practice of torture) reveals a desire for purity, an anxiety fueled by the impossibility of accessing the truth of the other. Specifically, it is the Greek notion of *alêtheia* as a buried truth brought to light, as unconcealment (in contrast to *nêmertes*, the unfailing, accurate truth of the underworld) that is at stake in the practice of torture. It is the secret of the other or, as I will argue, the "unrevealability"[3] of the truth of the other, that stands as the "real" motive for torture, as well as that which ensures torture's inevitable failure. (More will be said about this below, where I argue that torture can occasionally succeed at gathering facts but will always—in each and every case—fail to "solve" the mystery of the other.) In what follows I will demonstrate the way in which the marrano—as a subject constituted by a secret—stands as a powerful example of the dynamic that is at work in the use of violent interrogation. I suggest, finally, that torture itself can be understood as a sort of conversion: in the case of the marrano, a conversion of the already-converted other.

TORTURE AS CONVERSION

In the spring of 2004, 60 *Minutes* and *New Yorker* magazine broke the story of Abu Ghraib, releasing photographs that documented inhumane and illegal acts of torture committed by the U.S. military against Iraqi prisoners. The images shocked the world, and fierce debates ensued over who was to be held responsible: did the pictures reveal the actions of "a few bad apples," or was the implementation of torture directly or indirectly sanctioned by authorities leading all the way to the White House? A simultaneous conflict accompanied the legal or moral conflict: a battle over words. The illegally apprehended prisoners were called "detainees" (not prisoners of war) by officials; the wrongdoing resided in the "dissemination" of the digital images (rather than the violent acts depicted in the photographs); the acts were described as "abuse" (rather than torture).[4] Even more than in Guantánamo, the U.S. military failed to get any kind of useful intelligence in Abu Ghraib. This lack of intelligence was, counterintuitively, used to amplify the practice of torture; the less information the torture yielded, in fact, the more brutal the methods employed. This is because the existence of Abu Ghraib—a prison full of masses of predominantly innocent Iraqis—needed to be justified, a difficult goal that could only be accomplished through the dehumanization of these citizens. Through the use of torture, prisoners were turned into abject terrorists while the U.S. military was validated as an occupying power: violent interrogation doubly performed acts of conversion upon both prisoner and guard.

Scarry details the way in which this happens, arguing that torture fuctions as the means by which an unstable regime announces its own position by converting the language of the other into its own, that is, by doubling its voice. Relying on the radical inexpressibility of physical pain, torture mimics the "language-destroying capacity" of pain "in its interrogation, the purpose of which is not to elicit needed information but visibly to deconstruct the prisoner's voice" (*The Body in Pain*, 20). Scarry explains that "the physical pain is so incontestably real that it seems to confer its quality of 'incontestable reality' on that power that has brought it into being. It is, of course, precisely because the reality of that power is so highly contestable, the regime so unstable, that torture is being used" (27). This process is carried out through a double, contradictory movement that is at work in the infliction of physical pain as part of interrogation. Torture simultaneously depends upon the *concreteness* of the experience of physical pain as well as the *inexpressibility* of this experience. The torturer performs a kind of transference or reversal of these aspects of pain: the doubt associated with the *representability* of pain is used to destroy the prisoner's self, language, and world, while the "factualness" of the *sensation* of pain is borrowed in order to cement the (fabricated) truth of the regime.

Scarry's use of the motif of conversion to refer to the practice of torture—her central thesis details "the conversion of real pain into the fiction of power"—suggests an interdependent relation between the acts of conversion and torture, as well as the necessarily fictional nature of these acts. If torture itself behaves as a sort of conversion in which a confession is not extracted, but rather composed through the act of interrogation, and if this conversion is fashioned imaginatively (not unlike the writing of a narrative), then Scarry's reading of torture is doubly relevant to the present study. The converted Jews of early modern Spain and Portugal, many of whom were arrested, interrogated, and tortured by the Inquisition, are subjected to yet another process of conversion: the adaptation of their histories into art by the nineteenth- and twentieth-century works that seek to represent them.

Within the historical context of the Inquisition, the volatility of the signifier "marrano" appears intimately linked to another site of discursive instability: the scene of interrogation, which serves as both the literal and symbolic epicenter of the Inquisition (the objective of which, of course, is to question), and simultaneously contributes to and is fueled by the invention of the marrano (or converso) as untrustworthy subject. Because of the marrano's liminal position between Judaism and Christianity, which produces a deep-seated anxiety in the Old Christian subject, the interrogation becomes both a response to and condensation of this discomfort. If such a dynamic is already in play in antiquity, as duBois's account of ancient Athenian culture makes clear, it becomes radicalized through a figure that is not imagined in opposition to the self, as was the signifier "slave," but whose identity is radically indeterminate. It is not possible to uncover the "essence" of the New Christian, just as the "true beliefs" of the political prisoner under Southern Cone dictatorships or the alleged terrorist in Abu Ghraib remain outside the grasp of the torturer, not because of the stubbornness of the prisoner or inefficiency of the torturer, but due to the indeterminacy of "belief" itself. The interrogation of converted Jews by the Inquisition stands as a particularly illustrative case study because it demonstrates the defining traits of torture that I have outlined above: (1) it responds to the identitary instability of the New Christian subject, which eludes the established socioreligious categories of "Jew" and "Christian"; (2) it aims to produce the identitary purity lacking in both New Christian and Old; (3) it behaves as a kind of conversion that both reenacts and supplements the original conversion of Jew into Christian (the marrano's malleability ensures both the possibility and impossibility of this act); and (4) it creatively fashions the truth of an unstable regime. The thematization of this historical violence in works of fiction (narrative, drama, and film) in the nineteenth and twentieth centuries creates an alternate avenue into the debate over torture and truth by exposing the necessarily fictional quality of interrogation and confession, as well as by offering a supplementary poetic discourse that can either reproduce or deconstruct the bond between torture and truth. Yet the representation of violent interrogation in literature is not the only relationship between torture and art, as Slovenian political thinker Slavoj Žižek argues.

THE AESTHETICS OF TORTURE

In the preface to his 2005 *Interrogating the Real*, Žižek refers to the surprising discovery by a Spanish art historian that modernist art was used by anarchists in the torture of pro-Franco prisoners in Civil War Spain. Taking as their inspiration Kandinsky and Klee, Buñuel and Dalí, secret torture chambers were constructed in Barcelona in 1938 that forced Nationalist prisoners to confront dizzying images of colors and shapes, cubes, lines, and spirals, "tricks of colour, perspective and scale to cause mental confusion and distress" (8). Now, much has been said about the ambivalent relation between modernism and totalitarian thought: it is well-known that Hitler blamed the degeneration of German culture on modernist art, for example, though the opposite tendency can also be found, in which many modernists were themselves proto-fascists. In the case Žižek discusses, the Spanish anarchists played directly into the idea of abstract art as destructive, employed as a technique in the broader act of torture, the aim of which is to "unmake" the language, self, and world of the prisoner.

Žižek turns to the unexpected encounter—or misencounter—between so-called high culture and the vulgar brutality of torture in order to expose the gap between the two. The eternally parallel existence of the two phenomena, he insists, ensures that they can never coincide on a structural level: "revolutionary politics and revolutionary art move in different temporalities—although they are linked, they are two sides of the same phenomenon which, precisely as two sides, can never meet" (*Interrogating the Real*, 9–10). What is at stake here, in the unpacking of the impossible relationship between art and torture, between "high" aesthetics and "debased" political violence, is nothing less than the exposure of the Lacanian Real, the traumatic kernel that refuses symbolization.

While affirming Žižek's claim, I want to suggest that avant-garde movements such as surrealism and the act of torture have, in fact, more in common that one might initially suspect. Whether or not they actually ever meet, there is at work in each an impulse to dismantle the world of the other (of the spectator, of the prisoner). If Dalí, through his paintings, aims to subvert the preestablished ontological categories of the modern subject, so too does the torturer seek to unmake the "voice" and "world" of the torture victim.[5] This is Scarry's contention: in response to the lack of "positive" substance in the regime (a regime in crisis, though one can argue that any regime is by definition *always already* in crisis, or behaves as if in permanent crisis), the torturer implements pain, the concreteness of which compensates for the instability of the regime, in order to enact the erasure of the prisoner's world.[6]

What happens, then, when the work of art seeks to represent the act of torture, when torture itself is taken as the object of aesthetic interest? What ideas (of language, of self, of world) are preserved intact and what dismantled or reconfigured? Can an aesthetic work reproduce the logic of torture at the same time that it takes a critical stance against it? Put in Žižek's (Lacanian) terms, can art (theater, film, narrative) traverse the fantasy (*fantôme*) in order to confront the gap or void of the Real and its multiple representations? How might aesthetic or literary discourse point to the traumatic kernel at the heart of any construction of identity or truth *without* suturing the gap?

The 1967 film *The Battle of Algiers,* a pathbreaking documentary-style fictionalization of the Algerian struggle for independence from colonial domination, stands as, if not the first, certainly the best-known early instance of the use of cinema to take a political stand against the use of torture. The film opens with the stark black-and-white images of an imprisoned National Liberation Front (FLN) operative who has just been tortured: he appears to reside on the border between life and death or, perhaps more precisely, between opposing states of consciousness or subjectivity. Once a prominent leader of the armed uprising against the French, the prisoner has been reduced to a degraded informant who, in the following scene, leads the French occupiers to the secret hiding place of FLN leader Ali la Pointe.[7] Although the scene alludes to but does not show directly the acts of torture that have allowed his captors to extract this valuable information—the more brutal scenes come later in the film, after the story has been told from the beginning of the uprising—a crucial link is established from the outset between torture and truth.[8] The implied infliction of pain in conjunction with careful interrogation yields the desired results: the acquisition of information ("the truth") that will lead to the enemies' defeat.

The depiction of torture in *The Battle of Algiers* can be read as a political act insofar as it occupies an oppositional stance in relation to the practice. The film reveals abhorrent acts of violence to the viewing public and demands that this violence be named. In a press-conference scene halfway through the film, journalists politely and euphemistically probe Colonel Mathieu about the methods used to acquire information from prisoners until a more forthright journalist dares to pronounce the unmentionable word: "I feel that being excessively careful, my colleagues keep asking roundabout questions to which you can only reply in a roundabout way . . . If it's torture, let's speak of torture." Yet while the film stands in critical opposition to the use of torture by the French (even as the Colonel clarifies that he is an opponent of fascism and that, in fact, it is he who defended France against the Nazis just a decade earlier), the *revelation* of violence does little to dismantle the relationship between torture and truth. That is, although *The Battle of Algiers* takes a (political or moral) stance against the violation of these prisoners' rights, the idea of torture itself remains intact because it is still shown to *extract the truth:* the infliction of violence elicits a name, which is added to a chart that maps the structure of the FLN in order to eliminate its leadership. If the aesthetic resistance to torture can leave the practice unscathed, then, what would it look like for a work of art to subvert the act of torture, beyond simply naming it as wrong? In what way can literary language interrupt the seemingly necessary link between torture and truth, in the very place in which other discourses fall short? In what way can we begin to think about a logic of truth—an ethic of truth— that would disrupt the related practices of torture and conversion that constitute Inquisitional logic? Approached hauntologically, as we shall see, aesthetics can provide a way of understanding what truth is, and how the truth emerges and can be produced, that disrupts the way that Inquisitional logic links the production of truth, and the conceptualization of a truth so produced, to torture and to conversion.

In the chapters that follow, I address the above questions by focusing on four aspects of the aesthetic representation of Inquisitorial interrogation: the aporetic nature of *marranismo;* the allegorization of the Inquisition; literary scenes of interrogation and confession; and the ethics and politics of the aesthetization of torture. In the following two chapters on *marranismo* and allegory, I establish the foundation that allows me to understand the representations of torture and confession analyzed in the book's final two chapters. Specfically, I argue that the marrano (a subject understood to guard a secret) and allegory (a rhetorical tool thought to disguise the "true story" by speaking *otherwise*) bear a formal resemblance to interrogation, which is fueled by the desire to access the hidden truth of the other. By deconstructing the notion of *alêtheia* as hidden truth that stands at the heart of conventional understandings of *marranismo*, allegory, and torture—by reframing the idea of the secret as untranslatability, as radical singularity—it becomes possible to imagine the limits of Inquisitional logic.

Chapter 1 ("Aporias of *Marranismo*") takes as its point of departure Ricardo Forster's contention that the marrano exposes a broader chasm at the heart of the modern subject. Reflecting upon the historical phenomenon of crypto-Judaism or *marranismo* in early modern Iberian and colonial Latin American culture, this chapter analyzes the curious resurgence of marrano figures in nineteenth- and twentieth-century theater and film. These theatrical and cinematographic works, which shall serve as the principal corpus of the book, have as their protagonists two historical figures from early modern Luso-Hispanic culture, Luis de Carvajal and Antônio José da Silva. Both men belonged to crypto-Jewish families that undertook transatlantic crossings typical of marranos in the colonial period: while the Carvajals traveled from the Iberian Peninsula to New Spain in the sixteenth century in one of the early voyages of conquest in colonial Mexico, the da Silvas were uprooted from their native Brazil to be tried by the Inquisition in eighteenth-century Lisbon. The Carvajals and the da Silvas have captured the attention of a number of nineteenth- and twentieth-century Iberian and Latin American filmmakers, dramatists, novelists, and historians, who detect in their stories clues to the formation of modern ethnic, religious, and political subjectivities.

In my discussion of Mexican filmmaker Arturo Ripstein's 1974 *El Santo Oficio* and compatriot Sabina Berman's 1991 play *En el nombre de Dios* (both of which detail the Carvajal chronicle in colonial Mexico), together with Brazilian playwright Gonçalves de Magalhães's 1838 *O poeta e a inquisição*, Portuguese playwright Bernardo Santareno's 1966 *O Judeu* and Brazilian filmmaker Jom Tob Azulay's 1996 *O Judeu* (all of which explore the life of dramatist Antônio José da Silva), this chapter highlights the way in which figurative renderings of crypto-Judaism articulate a fundamental ambivalence surrounding *marranismo* and modern subjectivity. I turn to Jacques Derrida's work on secrecy and *marranismo* in order to argue that the aesthetic work oscillates between the thematization and subversion of the Cartesian subject through the aporetic figure of the marrano.

Chapter 2 ("Allegory and Hauntology") investigates the allegorical turn to the Inquisition during the second half of the twentieth century, during which time artists and intellectuals struggled to articulate the horror of fascist regimes on both sides of the Atlantic. These Inquisition narratives, I suggest, return to the foundational violence of the colonies (in Latin America) and the empire (in the case of Portugal) in order to address contemporary instantiations of political violence. I propose a reading that moves away from conventional understandings of the use of allegory under totalitarian governments—in which allegory is believed to disguise the "truth" out of fear of censorship (just as the marrano is typically understood as a subject that fashions a mask to conceal her "true" identity)—by turning to the work of Walter Benjamin and Jacques Derrida. Reading Benjamin's idea of the "death's head" (in *The Origin of German Tragic Drama*) together with Derrida's notion of the "specter" (in *Specters of Marx*), I demonstrate the way in which the remains of historical violence haunt the present through the literary.

In order to illustrate my theory of allegory as hauntology, I place three of the works analyzed in the previous chapter—Ripstein's *El Santo Oficio* and Berman's *En el nombre de Dios*, which project contemporary ethnic and class struggle in Mexico onto a sixteenth-century context, and Santareno's *O Judeu*, which links Inquisitorial violence to twentieth-century authoritarianism in Portugal—in juxtaposition with American playwright Arthur Miller's *The Crucible*, which critiques 1950s McCarthyism through the lens of the Salem Witch Trials. Calling into question the conventional notion of allegorical representation in the context of political repression, I propose a concept of allegory in which the ruins of history serve as both the condition of possibility and impossibility for contemporary readings of violence and totalitarianism.

After deconstructing the dynamic of masquerade proper to characterizations of both *marranismo* and allegory in the first and second chapters, I turn to scenes of torture and confession in chapter 3 ("Interrogative Signs"). The inherently discursive quality of interrogation and confession, as well as the subject that is constituted within the scene of torture, mark the central preoccupation of this chapter. In the first section, I trace the presence of confessional discourse through the realms of the legal, the literary, and the religious, in dialogue with Peter Brooks's recent book *Troubling Confessions*. Considering Brooks's argument that within the Western tradition, confession becomes the means by which the "individual authenticates his inner truth," together with Belgian critic Paul de Man's deconstructive reading of Rousseau's *Confessions* as exposure (in *Allegories of Reading*), I aim to highlight the decidedly literary quality of the confession, as well as of the narrative subject that is constituted through this performative act. If the confession is always already literary, what does the representation of the confession from the perspective of the literary do to our understanding of this practice? How do representations of marrano confession, in particular, contribute a previously overlooked dimension to discussions of the literary genre? In order to address these questions, I analyze several confessional scenes in Gonçalves de Magalhães, arguing that literary discourse can simultaneously profess innocence while performing guilt.

Finally, in what sense is the confession necessarily a response to the positing of a question? Can we understand the dynamic of interrogation as a form of ideological interpellation in an Althusserian sense? In what way is modern subjectivity premised upon the "turning" of the individual toward the Law, as in Louis Althusser's famous scene of hailing? In the second section of chapter 3, I consider the mutually interdependent acts of questioning and confession as a possible instantiation of what Michel Foucault and Judith Butler have characterized as the paradoxical relationship between subjection and subjectivation. Opening with a discussion of Franz Kafka's protagonist Josef K. in *The Trial*, I then turn to several scenes of Inquisitorial interrogation in Ripstein, Berman, and Azulay in order to reflect upon the way in which the marrano is constituted as a guilty subject. Through close readings of these torture scenes, I strive to highlight a common dynamic at play in conventional readings of *marranismo*, allegory, and interrogation: specifically, that the acts of conversion, allegorization, and torture all respond to the secret (which Derrida understands as the limit to absolute hegemony and state sovereignty) that resides at the heart of the other. This impossible presence (of identity, of meaning), I argue, haunts the historical practices of *marranismo*, allegory, and interrogation, as well as their representation in narrative, theater and film.

The concluding chapter of the book ("Other Inquisitions") tackles directly the blind spot of Inquisitional logic and the relationship between torture and truth. Here, I depart from the main corpus of Inquisition narratives and reflect more broadly upon the ethico-political dimension of torture and interrogation, as well as the aesthetic representation of these acts. In order to demonstrate the way in which literature approaches the problem of torture and truth from a unique perspective, this chapter considers the possibility of an "ethics of seeing" in José Saramago's 2004 *Ensaio sobre a Lucidez* (translated as *Seeing*), in which an unnamed government declares a state of emergency following the mysterious appearance of millions of blank votes during a national election. Through a close reading of three scenes of questioning, I consider the possibility of the deconstruction of interrogation through the literary. Engaging the notion of event in Jacques Derrida and Alain Badiou, I argue that Saramago subverts the "truth" of the lie detector by demonstrating that the event of truth (or the truth of the event) disrupts any intent to control information through interrogation. Placing Saramago's notion of "seeing" (*lucidez*) alongside Emmanuel Levinas's idea of "saying" (*le dire*), I conclude the book by considering how the literary can interrupt or sabotage Inquisitional logic.

CHAPTER 1

Aporias of *Marranismo*

Leer al marrano, en parte, significa leer la incompletitud del
hombre en la modernidad. (To read the marrano, in part,
means to read the incompleteness of man within modernity.)
—Ricardo Forster

[The] secret keeps the Marrano even before the Marrano
keeps it.
—Jacques Derrida

MARRANO SECRETS

Just months before the attacks on the World Trade Center and the Pentagon set off a series of reactionary foreign policy decisions—including
the establishment of black sites in undisclosed foreign locations and
prisons in Guantánamo and Abu Ghraib, resurrecting the practice of
violent interrogation as a primary means by which military and private
contractors attempted to extract the "truth" through torture—Peggy
Kamuf edited and translated a collection of essays by Jacques Derrida
on the topics of lying and truth-telling, alibis and confessions. *Without Alibi*, the introduction to which Kamuf completed in June 2001,
includes lectures delivered in the United States during the 1990s that
anticipate the urgent questions of the post-9/11 era: the relationship
between machine and event, truth and fiction, and the history of confession. In one of the volume's most provocative essays, "History of the
Lie: Prolegomena," Derrida develops a critical genealogy of lying—as
well as a genealogy of *thinking* about lying—by linking it structurally
to the concepts of *marranismo* and secrecy, underscoring the structural
untruth(s) that haunts every truth. To this specter Derrida gives the
name *marrano*.

Of course, debates on torture and confession, testimony and truth, had already permeated Latin Americanist circles for several decades, as intellectuals, journalists, and human rights activists responded to the brutality of the Southern Cone dictatorships, when state-sanctioned violent interrogation was used by the military and secret service to consolidate power and eliminate political resistance during the 1970s and 1980s. Yet while torture has been repudiated widely, it continues to be used not only by military regimes but also by ostensibly democratic governments. This is because, I want to suggest, the link between torture and truth—the classical idea that torture extracts the truth from the body of the other—is rarely called into question. Idelber Avelar has argued that until recently, social-scientific discourse has dominated conversations about torture, the proliferation of which is no longer doubted. What do literature and philosophy have to say about torture, asks Avelar, now that we no longer wonder whether or not torture happens? (Avelar, "Five Theses on Torture," 254).

The present chapter turns to a body of theatrical and cinematographic works from the nineteenth and twentieth centuries that return to the violent scene of the Inquisition and, in particular, to the families of two historical crypto-Jewish figures, Luis de Carvajal and Antônio José da Silva. Taking as my point of departure Derrida's reflections on *marranismo* and secrecy, I explore the aporetic nature of the marrano subject, arguing that it is the "universal" marrano that continues to inspire torture well beyond the historical confines of the Inquisition. By performing close readings of aesthetic representations of *marranismo* and crypto-Jewishness, by exposing what Latin American literary critic Patrick Dove calls the "enigmatic singularity of the text ... what is both in and more than the text's intentional, metaphorical signifying economy" (*Catastrophe of Modernity,* 22), I aim to destabilize ideas of subjectivity and truth that have served as the basis for torture from Greek antiquity to the present.

True Lies

Let us say that there is a secret here. Let us testify: There is
something secret. (*Il y a là du secret.*)
—Jacques Derrida

Initially delivered as a lecture at the New School for Social Research in 1994, Derrida's "History of the Lie" details the "frank," "decidable" definition of the lie that has permeated Western civilization in its various forms (Greek, Roman, Judaic, Christian, Islamic).[1] Simply put, lying has been understood as a meaning-to-say: that is, the deception rests in the speaker's *intention* to deceive more than the specific *content* of the lie, so that both lying and truth-telling incorporate a performative in addition to a constative dimension. Derrida's elaboration upon the constative and the performative responds to Paul de Man's deconstructive reading of Rousseau's *Confessions* in *Allegories of Reading,* in which the Belgian-born critic emphasizes the competing motives and desires that drive confessional discourse.[2] Complicating de Man's thesis, Derrida argues in favor of a history of the lie that would expose the mutual interdependence of the performative and the constative.[3] He suggests that even the notion of lying as event—in which a lie is performatively fashioned in relation to the (overlooked, forgotten, or intentionally ignored) promise of truth—seems to reproduce the stable, "square" idea of truth.

The marrano (a complex anti-identitary concept to which Derrida confesses an affinity)[4] participates not only in the history of the lie, but in the history of the secret. Citing Alexandre Koyré's idea of a public secret—a "political cryptology" or a "society with a secret" (Derrida, "History of the Lie," 63), which he likens to the mentality of the marrano—Derrida postulates the idea of the secret as a limit to absolute hegemony and state sovereignty.[5] He turns to the figure of the marrano in order to highlight the difficult rapport between lying and truth-telling, given the rocky history of marrano lies, marrano confessions, and—above all—marrano secrets.[6] Emphasizing the *structure* of the secret, rather than any alleged content, he highlights the stubborn persistence of the idea of hiddenness within the concept of the lie. For Derrida, the secret (and the marrano secret in particular) possesses no positive content, but rather exhibits the simultaneous presence-absence we find in the specter: "A specter is both visible and invisible, both phenomenal and nonphenomenal: a trace that marks the present with its absence in advance" (Derrida and Stiegler, *Echographies of Television,* 117).[7] In "Passions: An Oblique Offering," Derrida had already argued in favor of an idea of the secret that would resist the logic of *alêtheia,* or unburied truth, which has served as the foundation for torture since Greek antiquity. The secret exists (*"There is something secret"*), but it can neither be concealed nor unconcealed:

> Heterogeneous to the hidden, to the obscure, to the nocturnal, to the invisible, to what can be dissimulated and indeed

> to what is nonmanifest in general, [the secret] cannot be un-
> veiled. It remains inviolable even when one thinks one has
> revealed it. Not that it hides itself forever in an indecipher-
> able crypt or behind an absolute veil. It simply exceeds the
> play of veiling/unveiling, dissimulation/ revelation, night/day,
> forgetting/anamnesis, earth/heaven, etc. It does not belong
> therefore to the truth, neither to the truth as homoiosis or
> adequation, nor to the truth as memory (Mnemosyne, ale-
> theia), nor to the given truth, nor to the promised truth, nor
> to the inaccessible truth. (26)

Derrida is interested not so much in identifying historical instances of cultural *marranismo*—which he declares to be "finished" (*Aporias,* 74)—but rather in the marrano as metonym: "the metonymic and generalized figure of the Marrano, the right to secrecy as right to resistance against and beyond the order of the political" ("History of the Lie," 64). Kamuf rightly interprets Derrida's marrano not only as "a figure for absolute secrecy" but also as "a figure of resistance to or within the fiction of the legal subject" (13). Thus if the marrano stands for secrecy or resistance, by acknowledging the marrano's aporetic secret—by confronting the fact that the marrano has "nothing" to hide—it becomes possible to expose the fictionality of the legal subject, the fact that at the core of the modern subject of truth resides a lie.[8] This is why both confession (or truth-telling) *and* lying remain bound to the logic of proof, while the idea of testimony or bearing witness allows for the possibility of something else: an idea of inviolability that can be acknowledged even if it can neither be revealed nor proven through legal discourse.

So why talk about marranos now, in post-dictatorship Latin American and Iberian culture, as well as the post-9/11 era? What political or ethical demand could the specter of *marranismo* (itself always already spectral) make, and how does it pose such a demand? The present chapter takes Derrida's discussion of marranos, confessions, lies and secrets as a point of departure to analyze the aesthetic or figurative use of *marranismo* in nineteenth- and twentieth-century Latin American and Iberian film and theater. At stake in the analysis of the marrano and its representations, I argue, is nothing less than the exposure of the limits of modern subjectivity, sovereignty, and hegemony: Inquisitional logic in its various manifestations. After reflecting briefly upon the "finished" forms of marrano culture in order to consider the spectral trace it has left in its wake, I turn to fictional representations of Carvajal and da

Silva, asking what the literary or the aesthetic might contribute to debates on *marranismo* and secrecy, torture and truth.

Marranismo *and the Specter of Modernity*

El marrano es el alter ego del sujeto moderno, de ese sujeto
construido como univocidad alrededor del proyecto de una
racionalidad autosuficiente. (The marrano is the alter ego of
the modern subject, of that subject constructed as univocity
around the project of self-sufficient rationality.)
—Ricardo Forster

The waves of Jewish conversion beginning in late fourteenth-century Spain—over and above marking a fascinating, and violent, moment in early modern Iberian history—initiated the formation of a wholly new subject (one that is conflicted, divided, and guilt-ridden) in addition to announcing the contradictions and limits of an embryonic modernity and, in particular, of the emergent modern subject.[9] The Jews who—primarily in response to the popular pogroms of 1391 in Spain and the Spanish and Portuguese Edicts of Expulsion in 1492 and 1496—converted to Christianity by force or by free will, and who subsequently suppressed, transformed, observed clandestinely, or rejected Jewish rites and customs, came to assume a previously nonexistent identity, one in which the "public" and "private" selves were at odds, and in which even "internal" articulations of culture and religiosity were fraught with incongruity and ambivalence (Yovel, *The Other Within,* 344). The nascent marrano subject simultaneously represented the condition of possibility and impossibility of the constitution of the modern (Old Christian) subject, whose existence both depended upon and was threatened by the New Christian. Of course, the very origins of Christianity can be read as converso in nature: the birth of Christianity *necessarily involved* the conversion not only of Jews but of Judaism itself, so that Jewish conversion can be understood as that which allows for the existence of Christianity, at the very same time that it marks its limit.[10]

The mass conversion of Jews and the birth of a new segment of society (which Yovel likens to a "caste") in Spain and, soon after, in Portugal can be understood as both the cause and effect of the official expulsion of Jews who refused to convert. Indeed, Ferdinand and Isabella's expulsion of the Jews from Spain in 1492 can be read as an attempt to complete the conversion of New Christians by severing ties with their former coreligionists who provided necessary spiritual, material, and educational resources for the traditional, albeit secret, observance of Judaism. When the king and queen stated, in the Edict of Expulsion, that Spain must rid itself of Jews because "estos judíos tratan de todas maneras a subvertir la Santa Fe Católica y están tratando de obstaculizar cristianos creyentes de acercarse a sus creencias" (these Jews try in every way to subvert the Holy Catholic Faith and are trying to distance faithful Christians from their beliefs), they were responding to the nutritive relationship between Jews and *New* Christians, not Old Christians (traditional Jewish law would allow for the reconversion of former Jews but not of faithful Christians, who would be out of their jurisdiction). At the same time, New Christians were incorporated within the domain of the recently unified crown—on the brink of becoming a dominant colonial power—because they were considered necessary on a social, economic, and professional level. Yovel tells us that they were priests, soldiers, politicians, professors, judges, theologians, writers, poets, legal advisors, physicians, accountants, and traders (positions that had in part been occupied by Jews prior to their expulsion) and thus indispensable to the crown (*The Other Within*, 62).[11]

In addition to the paradoxical socioeconomic status of the New Christian in a newly reunified Spain, marrano identity came to both embody and inspire ambivalence in the dominant culture on a more psychic level, related at least in part to what Yovel terms "identity passions."[12] The Jewish convert to Christianity proved threatening because she exposed the tenuous divide between Jew and Christian, and between ideas of "self" and "other" more broadly. Sociologist Zygmunt Bauman discusses this dynamic within the context of European modernity, proposing the term "proteophobia" to explain ambivalence toward Jews: "the proper generic phenomenon of which the resentfulness of the Jews is a part is proteophobia, not heterophobia; the apprehension and vexation related not to something or someone disquieting through otherness and unfamiliarity, but to something or someone that does not fit the structure of the orderly world, does not fall easily into any of the established categories" (*Modernity and the Holocaust*, 144). According to Bauman, the assimilated Jew inspires anxiety in the modern European subject due to its resistance to classification. The early modern Jewish convert, as I have demonstrated in previous work, provokes a more extreme reaction by occupying an even less identifiable position and anticipates the later version of itself: the secular, assimilated Jew.[13]

In his discussion of the relationship between *marranismo* and modernity, Ricardo Forster argues that the marrano represents the alter ego of the modern subject, both because the fractured, incomplete marrano exposes the impossibility of the modern Cartesian subject's claim to wholeness, rationality, and autonomy, and because the marrano inhabits a crack in the decidedly modern project of colonial expansion: "El marrano representa el punto exacto en el que todo el esfuerzo del sujeto racional por desplegarse hegemónicamente en el centro de la escena histórica señala su anticipadora imposibilidad, la sombra inicial de su futura descomposición" ("The marrano represents the exact point at which all of the rational subject's efforts to insert himself hegemonically into the center of the historical scene signals its anticipatory impossibility, the initial shadow of its future decomposition") (Forster, "La aventura marrana," 154). The marrano subject matters to us—here, now—because it signals, from the beginning, the *other side* of reunification, nationalism, and colonialism, as well as the necessary failure of these political, religious, and identitary projects. *Marranismo* works on a number of levels, within distinct spheres (the cultural, the socioeconomic, the religious, the metaphysical, the political, the symbolic), and its effect can be felt across the Atlantic: not only because of the marrano participation in early voyages of conquest in the Americas, but also in light of the conversion and subjugation of indigenous communities in the colonies.[14]

The fact that conversos or New Christians (not Jews, as is frequently believed) served as the primary target of the Spanish and Portuguese Inquisitions—at least until the early part of the sixteenth century, after which time they were replaced by Alumbrados, spiritual seekers, and Lutherans (Yovel, *The Other Within*, 165)—supports the thesis that there is something uniquely threatening about the marrano. The Inquisition pursued heretics from within not simply due to a question of jurisdiction, but because, simply put, there was more at stake: this "other within" represented a major obstacle to the invention and preservation of the "pure" Christian subject (hence the establishment and reliance upon purity of blood statutes to determine a hierarchy within Iberian Christian society).

Forster's assertion, finally, that the marrano constitutes a "fiction" and that "la ficción marrana hace resistencia a esa otra ficción que constituye la línea maestra de la modernidad" ("the marrano fiction resists that other fiction that constitutes the dominant thread of modernity") is essential to the present study, which takes as its principal object of investigation creative works that thematize the marrano ("La aventura marrana," 153). If nineteenth- and twentieth-century works of art figuratively convert the *already converted* other of history into a contemporary literary motif, the *fictionalization* of the fiction "marrano"—a double or metacritical gesture—proves a fruitful object of analysis. What's more: the fictions discussed in this chapter belong to the genres of theater and film, in which the performative or theatrical quality of marrano identity is underscored through visual or dramatic media. What remains to be determined is whether the aesthetic performances in question open or foreclose reading *marranismo* in the sociohistorical, ideological, and aesthetic moments from which they emerge, as well as the myriad places to which they travel in unanticipated future readings.

I turn now to the marrano fictions that serve as the principal corpus for this book: theatrical and cinematographic works from the past two centuries, with a particular focus on those produced during the second half of the twentieth century that emerge during or in the wake of totalitarian regimes in Latin America and the Iberian Peninsula.[15] These plays and films have as their protagonists two marrano figures from colonial Mexico and early modern Portugal: Luis de Carvajal *el Mozo* (the Younger) and Antônio José da Silva (nicknamed *o Judeu,* or "the Jew"). The heterodox figure of Luis de Carvajal has captured the attention of a number of artists and historians in Mexico, in particular during the latter part of the twentieth century. Described by Yirmiyahu Yovel as "a mixture of quasi-biblical Jew, Jewish Alumbrado, semi-Karaite, and Christian-inspired scholastic . . . a martyr of a religion in which most rabbis would have felt strangers" (*The Other Within,* 319), *el Mozo* undertook, in the sixteenth century, a series of literal and figurative conversions to Christianity and back to Judaism that have been aesthetically represented in Mexican filmmaker Arturo Ripstein's *El Santo Oficio* (1974) and Mexican playwright Sabina Berman's *En el nombre de Dios* (1991). Antônio José da Silva, a Brazilian-Portuguese New Christian known for his satirical puppet operas in early eighteenth-century Lisbon (and who was ultimately murdered along with his family by the Inquisition), has piqued the interest of a number of artists from throughout the Lusophone world: Brazilian playwright Gonçalves de Magalhães's 1838 *O poeta e a inquisição,* Portuguese playwright Bernardo Santareno's 1966 *O Judeu,* and Brazilian Jom Tob Azulay's 1996 film of the same name.[16] Through the analysis of the aesthetic works that dramatize the lives of Carvajal and da Silva, I aim to deconstruct the aporetic nature of *marranismo* through the tropes of disguise and secrecy, puppetry and performance, in which we can find a persistent tension between assimilation and resistance, identification and refusal. In my discussion of the aesthetic "reconversion" of these historical figures, I aim to establish the foundation for a more profound reflection upon the allegorical quality of these works in chapter 2, as well as the relationship between conversion, confession, and torture in chapter 3.

EL MOZO AND MEXICAN MARRANISMO

The Carvajals, a wealthy family of crypto-Jews that arrived in New Spain in the sixteenth century, have been the subject of a number of historiographic and fictional works over the last century and a half, beginning with the publication of Vicente Riva Palacio's *El libro rojo* in 1871. As part of the landowning Peninsular elite, the Carvajals, with Luis de Carvajal the Elder as its patriarch, played a role in colonial Mexico not unlike that of many influential New Christians in Spain and Portugal at the time: a necessary but threatening element of the local elite that was at once vital and detrimental to the Old Christian religious and secular ruling class. The particular mode in which the family became inextricably tied to the ethnic, economic, and political conflicts of the period—culminating in the arrest and subsequent murder of the entire clan at the hands of the Inquisition—means that to "write" the Carvajals amounts to nothing less than an appraisal of the vast, intricate web of power at work at the time. In my discussion of Ripstein's and Berman's representations of Luis de Carvajal the Younger—the patriarch's nephew and successor, whose multiple and multidirectional conversions allow him to function as a blank screen onto which distinct aesthetic, social, and political concerns can be projected—I argue that the aesthetic work betrays a fundamental ambivalence toward *marranismo,* oscillating between the reproduction and deconstruction of the Cartesian subject through the aporetic figure of the marrano.

Arturo Ripstein's El Santo Oficio

In 1974, internationally renowned filmmaker Arturo Ripstein debuted *El Santo Oficio (The Holy Office),* the screenplay of which he penned in collaboration with poet, essayist, novelist, and fabulist José Emilio Pacheco, and which was entered into the 1974 Cannes Film Festival.

Ripstein, whose career was launched when he worked as an assistant to Luis Buñuel and whose film credits total nearly 200, adapted to film works by a number of major Latin American writers of the twentieth century such as Pacheco, Gabriel García Márquez, Carlos Fuentes, and José Donoso. Shot in a realist style and exemplifying both the sobriety and melodrama emblematic of Ripstein's work, *El Santo Oficio* aims to re-create the political, religious, and ethnic conflicts of the early colonial period in Mexico.[17]

The film opens with the funeral of Luis the Younger's father Rodrigo, whose death serves as the condition of possibility for the relationship between don Luis the Elder and his successor: indeed, Luis's name, as I shall discuss in my analysis of Berman's play, stems from the adoption of this substitute paternal figure who will guarantee a future of wealth and power for the young Carvajal. Death frames the plot—it marks both the commencement and the end of the Carvajal chronicle in colonial Mexico—and subsequently imbues with meaning everything that is contained within these mortal parentheses. The scene of the funeral is central to the depiction of the family and their community as clandestine Judaizers, establishing from the outset a rather uncomplicated opposition between public (Catholic) and private (Jewish). The screenplay specifies that Fray Gaspar de Carvajal (the only of Rodrigo's sons sent away to be raised by Dominicans, likely a conscious choice made to protect the family's reputation as "authentically" New Christian) acts as officiant, despite the fact that Doctor Antonio Morales, who serves as the rabbi to the underground community of crypto-Jews, is also in attendance. Gaspar appears confused that none of the mourners responds "Amen" to his Latin prayer, and reacts in horror when he overhears Morales quietly leading the group in a Hebrew blessing moments later.

From the beginning, then, the film portrays the Carvajals and their community as leading a double existence. Ripstein develops this tension further in the scene that follows, in which the family leaves the church grounds in order to observe Jewish rites of mourning in the privacy of their home. The content of what takes place in the opening scenes is communicated through setting: the Catholic funeral rites take place outdoors, while the crypto-Jewish practices occur behind closed doors. Indeed, once at home, a window is opened and immediately closed as if to remind the viewer of this vital barrier between interior and exterior, while simultaneously hinting that the divide may be more tenuous than it appears. This oppositional relationship between public and private, while ostensibly signaling a sort of religious syncretism, in fact maintains a clear boundary between the two religious worlds for much of the film. Luis the Younger serves as the one character who moves beyond the dichotomy between public and private, Catholic and Jewish in the heterodox brand of *marranismo* that he practices, signaling a fissure at the root of the New (and therefore Old) Christian subject.

The morbidity with which the film opens effectively foreshadows the fate of the Carvajal family, which turns out to be decided by the foolish observance of Jewish rites in front of Fray Gaspar (who, in his guilt and confusion, denounces his crypto-Jewish brethren to his confessor). The remainder of the film's plot focuses on the arrest, interrogation, and ultimate death of the entire Carvajal clan and their community. On the road to his ultimate demise, Luis undertakes a series of conversions (of himself and others) that together constitute him as an overconverted subject: a "super-"converso whose uncanny identity, language, and behavior complicate the dominant discourse of the film. The contradictory quality of Luis's *marranismo* culminates in a brutal scene of self-circumcision that, as I argue following a Derridean reading of the ancient ritual, reveals the necessarily aporetic nature of marrano subjectivity.

Together with his cellmate, Fray Hernando, Luis undergoes a spiritual reawakening that has more in common with Christian rebirth than anything found in the Jewish Talmudic tradition. While incarcerated, he first attempts to hide his mysterious spiritual musings—he scribbles secret messages onto avocado skins while murmuring inaudibly—but soon gives way to his cellmate's questions. Fray Hernando, the deranged monk who has been placed in Luis's cell in order to spy on him to acquire proof of his heresy, begins to attack his beliefs but soon finds himself swayed by the mystical prisoner's arguments. The debate between the two inmates embodies, to a degree, the theological clash that takes place within the marrano as well as more broadly within Iberian society, both on the Peninsula and in the colonies. That the transatlantic tension between New and Old Christian is played out through the relationship between a crypto-Jew and a mentally ill monk betrays an instability at the heart of the colonial Christian subject. Fray Hernando confesses that he has been placed in his cell as a spy, but assures him that he has not told the authorities anything because Luis's faith has moved him: "quisiera tener la fe que tú tienes" ("I want to have the faith that you have") (Ripstein and Pacheco, *El Santo Oficio*, 44).[18] Ironically, then, it is within the space of incarceration—ostensibly a site of repentance and reform—that Jews are "made"; indeed, Fray Hernando's conversion is immediately followed by that of Luis himself. Upon hearing the cries of his mother emanating from the walls of the torture chamber, *el Mozo* tells his companion that he has had a vision, and that his name is no longer Luis de Carvajal, but José Lumbroso: "'el que alumbra', 'el que arde en su fe'" ("he who illuminates, he who burns in his faith"), to which Fray Hernando responds by praying in Hebrew (56). The double conversion of the mad Catholic and the already converted Luis establishes the protagonist as a source of divine (if heterodox) truth within the scope of the film, although this truth will later be called into question.

Luis's spiritual awakening is followed by the realization of a third conversion: this one self-inflicted. After Luis is freed from prison on the condition that he renounce Judaism, wear a *sambenito* (penitential garment), and work assisting a priest in a mental institution, he is given the task of transcribing and translating religious texts, which he uses as a pretext to study the Hebrew Bible behind closed doors (reading the Bible was, of course, prohibited among Catholic laypeople). The film shows Luis reading the passage detailing the commandment that Jewish males be circumcised as proof of their covenant with God: "Y el varón incircunciso ... el que no circuncidare la carne de su prepucio ... será excluído de mi pueblo ... por haber violado mi pacto" ("And the uncircumcised male ... he who does not circumcise the flesh of his foreskin ... shall be excluded from my people ... for having violated my pact") (Ripstein and Pacheco, *El Santo Oficio*, 61). Luis realizes what he must do and—in a scene whose visual and aural brutality exceeds those representing the rape and torture of his mother and sister—violently removes his own foreskin with a pair of stolen scissors. This act, which he believes will officially return him to his faith and his God, marks his flesh as incontrovertibly other, a sign that anticipates the fate of his Judaizing family.

Over and above signaling the certain death of the crypto-Jewish Carvajals, Luis's self-circumcision also functions as a trope for the necessarily aporetic character of *marranismo:* the wounding of his own flesh simultaneously serves as the condition of possibility and impossibility of identity.[19] On the one hand, the cutting founds identity: Luis's Jewishness is determined *at the precise moment* in which he incises his flesh. Yet at the same time, the possibility of Luis's Jewishness is foreclosed by this act, particularly if we are to understand his auto-circumcision as Catholic sacrifice, following Deborah Bensadon's reading of the scene.[20] This aporia is fundamental not only to marrano circumcision but to the biblical origins of the practice of circumcision for all Jewish males.

The commandment that the Jewish male be circumcised as a sign of his covenant with God is worded in the following manner: he who is not circumcised (יִמּוֹל or "cut") will be excluded (וְנִכְרְתָה or "cut off") from my people (Gen. 17:14). Circumcision can therefore be interpreted as an act that cuts both ways, as a wounding that brings together as it divides, that separates as it binds. Derrida has written about circumcision as an ethical crime: ethical insofar as the act opens the same to the wholly Other (God), but which simultaneously serves to split the same from the other (those not counted among His people).[21] I would like to go a step further and suggest that circumcision does not merely bind one to the wholly Other (God) at the expense of the other (non-Jew), but that it establishes a porous border—a site of simultaneous passage and non-passage—that necessarily must be traversed. Circumcision in general, and marrano circumcision in particular, crystalizes the dynamic of the marrano and, by extension, of the modern subject: an aporetic subject whose wholeness is always already pierced by a shard of alterity.

In the film, however, the scene of circumcision does not succeed in binding Luis to his people at the expense of the other, as might be expected. His newfound faith translates into a decidedly non-Jewish desire to convert those around him, represented in *El Santo Oficio* with a critical, even ironic, distance. On the road to consult the hermit Gregorio López (another marginalized mystic), Luis encounters a group of indigenous men and boys who, like the Jews, have been converted to Christianity. He attempts to pursuade the group, whom he meets on their way to church, of the "truth," only to find that his efforts are in vain:

Luis: ¿Adónde van?

Joven: A la iglesia, a ver a Diosito. Hay epidemia.

Luis: Dios no está en las iglesias. La verdad es otra. A ustedes los sojuzgan y les imponen falsas creencias.

El joven ríe sin entender las palabras de Luis. El resto del grupo lo observa con desconfianza.

Luis: Les quitaron todo y les inculcan mentiras para hacerlos pensar como ellos. Quieren abusar y humillarlos a su antojo. La tierra es de ustedes. Así lo dispuso Adonay, único Dios verdadero. ¿Y qué les queda?: Ellos los condenaron a miseria, hambre y humillaciones.

Luis pretende compartir su panal con los indígenas. Ellos se alejan sin decir nada. (Ripstein and Pacheco, *El Santo Oficio*, 84)

Luis: Where are you going?

Boy: To church, to see God. There is an epidemic.

Luis: God cannot be found in the churches. The truth lies elsewhere. They enslave you and impose false beliefs on you.

The young boy laughs, not understanding Luis's words. The rest of the group observes him with suspicion.

Luis: They stole everything from you and they teach you lies to make you think like them. They want to abuse and humiliate you at their whim. The land is yours. That is the way Adonay, the only true God, made it. And what are you left with? They condemned you to misery, hunger and humiliations.

Luis tries to share his honeycomb with the Indians. They move away without saying anything.

The scene of misunderstanding signals a double failure: the impossibility of communication between the Peninsulars and the indigenous, as well as the futility of Luis's self-appointed mission of de-proselytization. Indeed, his only "successful" convert is insane, revealing the preposterous quality of his missionary work, the necessarily flawed nature of the process of conversion itself and, ultimately, the inaccessibility or untranslatability of the "truth": the truth of the identity of the marrano, the truth of the other, the truth *as* other ("la verdad es otra," he sermonizes). Finally, the exchange between Luis and the Indians—the highly politicized quality of which I will analyze in the following chapter—suggests that the dynamic of conversion reaches far beyond the marrano community, revealing the inextricable link between Inquisition and conquest.

Luis's last attempt to "deconvert" or "reconvert" the other—this time, a fellow New Christian on his deathbed—turns out to be the act that seals his fate and lands him back in the Inquisitorial prison. Aware that he is condemned to die but hoping to avoid torture, Luis confesses that he is a Jew. He then converts two more times before his death: he repents in order to avoid being burned alive at the stake, but at the very moment of his death pronounces the first word of the Hebrew prayer ("*Shemá* . . .") in order to die a Jew. The multiple—one might say excessive—conversions of Luis throughout the film highlight the slippery, malleable nature of *marranismo*. At the same time, Luis's superficial oscillations between Judaism and Christianity expose a gap between—and within—external and internal identity or belief. What appears in many scenes of the film as the existence of Jewish belief or practice hidden beneath a falsely projected Christian façade is called into question by the protagonist's contradictory deeds, his atypically visible "Jewishness" (which contrasts with the rest of the crypto-Jewish community), as well as his failed project of Jewish proselytization. At once a convert and proselytizer, scribe and born-again, public Judaizer and heterodox mystic, Luis's behavior reveals the tenuous divide between Judaism and Christianity as impossible, suggesting that the marrano signals the birth of a paradoxical subject in the early stages of formation in colonial Mexico, a subject whose very existence is accompanied by its inevitable limit.

Sabina Berman's En el nombre de Dios

Berman's *En el nombre de Dios* (*In the Name of God*)[22] revisits the Carvajal story in an unorthodox tragicomedy that incorporates violence and flamenco, sex and death, *chichimecas* and Jews, offering a highly original reading of the crypto-Jewish family as well as the broader sociopolitical context from which they emerge, the consequences of which continue to affect contemporary Mexico. The work of the playwright, poet, psychologist, novelist, film director, essayist, and journalist, perhaps best known for her commercially successful *Entre Villa y una mujer desnuda* (*Between Pancho Villa and a Naked Woman*), has been celebrated for its irreverent humor and poetic approach to questions of sexuality, identity, culture, and politics. Many of her plays are concerned with masks, disguises, poses, and theatricality: in *El bigote* (*The Moustache*), to give but one example, an effeminate husband and masculine wife share a false moustache, which they alternately use to seduce women and repel would-be male suitors. In the metatheatrical *En el nombre de Dios*, Berman once again turns her attention to the trope of disguise, this time through the highly performative figure of the marrano.

Unlike Ripstein's film, Berman's play does not seek to reproduce authentically the historical period in which the Carvajal story takes place. The stage directions indicate that the set "shouldn't attempt faithful realism," the dialogue approximates twentieth-, rather than sixteenth-century idiom, and anachronism is employed with liberal poetic license. *En el nombre de Dios* departs from the very literal presentation of historical material and plot in *El Santo Oficio,* which Berman imbues with complexity, paradox, poetry, and hybridity of genre. She intersperses dialogue with traditional *cante hondo,* flamenco dancing, and *palma-das,* which disrupt the fluidity of plot and scene in addition to conveying more depth of feeling. Finally, while the emotional spectrum in Ripstein's film remains restricted to sobriety and suffering, Berman opts to convey a broad range of affective experience spanning from joy to anguish as it vacillates abruptly between comedy and tragedy.

The preoccupation with naming and identity is present from the opening scene, which depicts the torture of an alleged crypto-Jew by the Inquisition. The interrogation scene does not focus on the clandestine (tangible, material) practice of Judaizing, as was typical of the Inquisitorial process, but rather on the prisoner's "secret" identity:

> *Inquisidor:* Tu nombre secreto.
>
> *Hombre:* Jorge Almeida.
>
> *Inquisidor:* He dicho tu nombre secreto.
>
> *Hombre:* Jorge Almeida.
>
> *Inquisidor:* ¡Tu nombre secreto!
>
> *Hombre:* . . .
>
> *Verdugo:* Pierde el aliento.
>
> *Inquisidor (indiferente):* Denle. Denle. Denle. (Berman, *En el nombre de Dios,* 331)

> *Inquisitor:* Your secret name.
>
> *Man:* Jorge Almeida.
>
> *Inquisitor:* I said, your secret name.
>
> *Man:* Jorge Almeida.
>
> *Inquisitor:* Your secret name!
>
> *Man:* . . .
>
> *Verdugo:* He can't breathe.
>
> *Inquisitor (indifferent):* Give it to him. Give it to him. Give it to him.[23]

This theatrical scene of interrogation, in which the lash of the *verdugo*'s whip is echoed by the stamping of the chorus's feet that evolves into a flamenco rhythm, does not attempt a realist mimesis of Inquisitorial questioning and confession. In this sense, the scene departs from many modern-day Inquisition narratives, which unwittingly reproduce Inquisitional logic even as they strive to resist it. Berman's torture scene, in contrast, goes directly to the (nonliteral) heart of the matter: the Inquisition is concerned with the secret that lies at the core of the identity of the other, a secret that is ultimately, fundamentally unreadable, signaled by the elliptical silence in place of a response. The marrano, we recall, is a subject that guards a secret par excellence: not secret as positive content (i.e., the clandestine practice of a particular Jewish custom or rite) but rather as form, or as empty form, as ellipsis. This is perhaps why for Derrida, the notion of the secret is always a double secret: the secret conceals another secret, the fact that the "secret" can neither be concealed nor revealed because it exceeds the logic of *alêtheia* as unburied truth.

The response of Jorge Almeida seems to state two things at once: there is a secret (name), and there is no secret (name). This is why Luisito's hybridity in Berman, as we see below, is more than a transgression of Judaism, or of Christianity, or of both: it is a transgression of the very logic of the Inquisition, the logic that founds all identity. Almeida's performative refusal to confess his secret name rejects the idea of the secret as positive content by refusing the terms of the interrogation. This is of course the ultimate transgression, the denial of the existence of identity as such in favor of the logic of the secret in the Derridean sense: untranslatable singularity. More than a signifier of emptiness, then, the ellipsis signals the gap or breach at the heart of every process of subjectivation/identification.[24] By articulating this idea through the medium of theater, Berman's dramatic discourse supplements philosophical discourse by infusing the elements of time and performativity into the idea of the secret as refusal: the untranslatable (proper) name of the crypto-Jew cannot be confessed but can only be resisted through active silence. Here, the crypto-Jew in particular and the crypto-subject in general bears a secret that is constitutive of his identity while at the very same time making identity impossible.

While Ripstein's and Berman's representations of the Carvajal plight differ in a number of significant ways, both are interested in the identitary elasticity of Luis *el Mozo* (dubbed "Luisito" in *En el nombre de Dios*). Berman opts to portray the adoption of Luis the Younger as his successor by Luis the Elder as a kind of conversion that echoes the religious oscillations of the protagonist. The relationship between Don Luis and Luisito—as well as the identity of the latter—relies upon the fluidity and ease with which he changes his name, saying "Yo no entiendo qué tanto puede importar un nombre. Es no más un poco de ruido" ("I don't understand what's so important about a name. It's just a bit of noise") (Berman, *En el nombre de Dios*, 339). Renouncing the name of his father in favor of that of his uncle and predecessor, Luisito unhinges what is conventionally understood as a fixed relationship between name and identity, signifier and signified.[25] The mutability of Luisito's name indicates a broader malleability of character: his heresy is understood as a transgression not merely of Catholic doctrine, but also of the Jewish traditions practiced by his relatives, as well as of identity more broadly. Viviana accuses him in front of the family of being a gypsy: "Luis baila como gitano. Me lo dijo mi tío Luis. Es tan flamenco que le llaman el Alumbrao. ¡Anda, Alumbrao! Así" ("Luis dances like a gypsy. My uncle Luis told me. He's so flamenco that they call him Alumbrao. Go, Alumbrao! Like that") (345). Later, in Jojutla, the family attorney declares his actions doubly heretical, a transgression against both Catholicism and Judaism: "Incontestablemente, herejía. Joder, hasta un rabino lo llamaría herejía" ("Indisputably, heresy. Fuck, even a rabbi would call it heresy") (372).

Like Ripstein, Berman includes the decisive scene of circumcision, but chooses to approach the event with humor, rather than violence. If in Ripstein, Luis's self-circumcision is represented as equally violent as the rape and torture of his mother and sister, in Berman the scene is imbued with a sort of pubescent humor. Strolling with *el Mozo*, Viviana reads him the biblical passage that commands the circumcision of Jewish males. She stumbles over the word "circumcised" (which she does not comprehend), her stuttering voice serving as hesitant narrator of the actions of Luisito. The command to cut, here, is itself cut by Viviana's stutter: the crypto-Jew's distance from Judaism, her ignorance, exposes the opening or wound that is present in this constitutive identitary act. Viviana's lack of knowledge, her not-knowing, takes the form of the comedic, undermining the solemnity of the act.

> *Luis desenvaina su cuchillo. Allí, está de espaldas, las piernas separadas.*
>
> *Viviana:* ¿Qué haces?
>
> *El Mozo:* No te vuelvas.
>
> *Viviana:* Ah, ya sé: mea. (*Retrocede unas páginas. Lee.*) "Y siendo Abraham de e-dad de no-venta y nueve años, Jehova le apareció y dijo-le: yo soy el Dios, todo-poderoso; anda delan-te de mí y sé perfe-, perfecto." "Anda delante de mí y sé perfecto."

La espalda de Luis se yergue. Luis clava en el piso el cuchillo. Entran voces cuchicheadas.

Coro: Mazal Tov. Buena suerte. Felicidades. (Berman, *En el nombre de Dios*, 347)

Luis unsheathes his knife. He stands with his back turned and spreads his legs.

Viviana: What are you doing?

El Mozo: Don't turn around.

Viviana: Oh, I know: you're peeing. (*She flips back a few pages. Reads.*) "And when Abraham was ninety-nine years o-old, Jehovah came to him and said to him: "I am God, the all-powerful; walk before me and be per- , perfect. Walk before me and be perfect."

Luis's back straightens. Throws the knife into the ground. Whispered voices are heard.

Coro: Mazal Tov. Good luck. Congratulations.[26]

The juxtaposition of what is meant to be a solemn ritual with Viviana's naïveté ("Oh I know: you're peeing") inflects Luisito's religiosity with an irreverence that undermines a more essentialist notion of Jewishness. The chorus's muted cries of congratulations that close the scene are then echoed as the next scene—a wedding scene—opens, cementing the union of ostensible opposites. Levity and sobriety, joy and mutilation are presented neither as discrete categories, nor as harmoniously syncretized elements, but rather as a necessary conjugation of humor and discomfort. While Berman's comedic approach diverges from the brutality of Ripstein, both scenes bear witness to the impossibility of the sovereign subject: Luis's self-circumcision exposes the fractured nature of his Jewishness as well as of *any* identitary cohesion.

Luisito's Jewishness, full of paradox and unease, is further called into question after the death of his father, at which point he confesses to his Catholic brother (whom Berman names Agustín, rather than Gaspar) the internal conflict he has inherited from his father. Fray Agustín convinces Luisito to accompany him to Jojutla in order to teach the local Indians to read and write.[27] Luisito agrees, and we next see him in Jojutla during Holy Week, at which time he is visited by Felipe Nuñez and the family lawyer. The scene in Jojutla functions as a staging of a theory of marrano identity, as well as of identity in general: "El pueblo entero de Jojutla era un teatro," relates Nuñez with unease, "en las calles se paseaban los indios vestidos de romanos (" . . . la iglesia estaba tam- bién repleta de indios . . . vestidos igualmente de romanos o de gente de la Jerusalén antigua" ("the whole town of Jojutla was a theater . . . Indians dressed as Romans wandered through the streets . . . the church was full of Indians . . . dressed as Romans or as people from ancient Jerusalem") (Berman, *En el nombre de Dios,* 368). The costumed mass of Indians produces in Felipe a feeling of profound disquiet: not only as a result of being one of the few Peninsulars in town, but because of the unsettling array of disguises. The radical theatricality culminates in the arrival of Luisito dressed as Jesus carrying a cross, singing a hymn "con aire flamenco" ("with a flamenco air") (371). Over and above standing as an example of colonial religious syncretism, Berman's representation of Holy Week in Jojutla postulates a theory of identity as performance that, rather than being concerned with the essence or interiority of the crypto-Jew, remains focused on the external, public, visual, and visible iterations of identity, iterations that are necessarily accompanied by the horror of the uncanny.

It is not a coincidence that Berman would explore questions of iden- tity and performance through the genre of theater, although as Samuel Weber argues in *Theatricality as Medium,* the phenomenon of theatrical- ity need not be confined to the dramatic genre. Yet while "theatricality" as event can in principle "take place" anywhere, theater permits us to find new names for retrograde notions of identity: "In the wake of the exhaustion of a conceptual tradition based on a certain notion of iden- tity, reflexivity, and subjectivity," Weber explains, "theater and theatri- cality emerge as names for an alternative that begins to articulate itself in the writings of [Kierkegaard, Marx, Nietzsche, Brecht, Artaud, De- leuze, Barthes, and Derrida]" (*Theatricality as Medium,* 2). The very his- tory of theater is riddled with tension between identity as self-reflexivity and that which would exceed the idea of *alêtheia* as unburied truth: "an alternative approach to the dominant Western concept of theater is already at work within the elaboration of the mainstream concept. It is not something simply imposed upon it from without, but accompanies it from the start" (2). In this sense, the problem of theatricality parallels the problem of *marranismo:* both oscillate historically and intertextu- ally between a performance that is "revealed" by a parting of curtains, and one that renders the separation between curtain and stage irrelevant, an idea of theatricality as event that resides in the "fold" of the curtain itself, in the differential repetition of the theatrical work: "Out of the dislocations of its repetitions emerges nothing more or less than the *singularity of the theatrical event.* Such theatrical singularity haunts and taunts the Western dream of self-identity" (7).

Like Ripstein's film, Berman's play concludes with the execution and burning of the entire Carvajal family, a highly theatrical public rite that adds a tragic dimension to the comedic work. That Berman opts to bring tragedy and comedy together reaffirms the multiple instantiations of conflict and paradox in the play. More than a sense of hybridity or a hybridity of sense, then, we are left with the notion that identity as performance is neither concealable nor revealable, much like the "secret name" the Inquisitors so desperately seek to learn in the opening scene. Returning to Derrida, the marrano, in Berman, does not keep a secret: rather, the secret keeps the marrano. If we can define the marrano (figuratively speaking) as "anyone who remains faithful to a secret that he has not chosen, in the very place where he lives, in the home of the inhabitant or of the occupant, in the home of the first or of the second arrivant, in the very place where he stays without saying no but without identifying himself as belonging to" (Derrida, *Aporias,* 81), then we can understand Berman's work as fundamentally ethical. In denying the confession of the secret name, in refusing to articulate a positive essence beneath or beyond performativity, *En el nombre de Dios* signals the unpronounceability of the name (*el nombre*), that is, the impossibility of identity that stands as its only possibility.

MARRANO AS MARIONETTE: INTERPRETING *O JUDEU*

While the Carvajal clan traveled together from the Old World to the New as part of an effort to colonize and populate New Spain in the sixteenth century, Antônio José da Silva's family was violently uprooted from Rio de Janeiro as they accompanied his mother, Lorença Coutinho, who was arrested and brought to Lisbon in order to be tried by the Inquisition at the beginning of the eighteenth century. The modern literary representations of the playwright's life have been equally mobile: historically, geographically, aesthetically, and ideologically. Domingos José Gonçalves de Magalhães's 1838 play *O poeta e a inquisição,* Camilo Castelo Branco's 1866 novel *O Judeu* (which I will not discuss here), Bernardo Santareno's 1966 dramatic narrative, also titled *O Judeu,* as well as Jom Tob Azulay's 1996 film of the same name, all revisit the life of da Silva and, in doing so, translate or "convert" his story into art.

The fact that his overdetermined nickname is chosen as the title for three of the four works in question demonstrates the way in which the aesthetic mimics the historical conversion of the Jewish other (or, conversely, the Judaizing of the New Christian other). Da Silva's "Jewishness"—or the idea of his "Jewishness"—is rhetorically vital to each textual project of imagining identity and difference, totalitarianism and violence. While da Silva, in these works, does not himself "flip-flop" between Judaism and Christianity in the way that Carvajal is shown to, the creative works themselves vacillate, converting and reconverting the historical figure of Antônio José, who appears alternatively as Jew, Christian, and atheist, tragic victim and principled hero, romantic subject and intellectual, depending upon the historical, political, and aesthetic context within which the work is produced. In addition to (re)converting the puppeteer himself, Magalhães, Castelo Branco, Santareno, and Azulay read da Silva's puppet operas in divergent and often contrasting ways, although it is Azulay who exploits most profoundly the link between marrano and marionette. I conclude the chapter by turning to Paul de Man's essay "Aesthetic Formalization: Kleist's *Über das Marionettentheater*," reflecting upon the rapport between *marranismo* and puppetry in relation to the question of mimesis.

Gonçalves de Magalhães's O poeta e a inquisição

Domingos José Gonçalves de Magalhães's 1838 *O poeta e a inquisição*—the debut of which at the Teatro Constitucional Fluminense has been credited with the inauguration of Brazilian romantic theater[28]—serves as a meditation on tragic fate, the relationship between interiority and subjectivity, as well as the very genre of theater itself. The first modern work of art to thematize the life and death of da Silva, *O poeta e a inquisição* paints the Brazilian-Portuguese artist as a persecuted crypto-Jew, downplaying the alternatively Christian, secular, and heterodox characteristics we will witness in the other works on the playwright. I want to explore the way in which marrano subjectivity is imagined in the play as linked to a notion of interiority that constitutes the modern subject while simultaneously signaling its limit. I argue that the idea of "truth" is intimately bound to a notion of the inner self that enjoys particular prominence in the tradition of romantic theater. Turning to critic Gabriela Basterra's work on tragic subjectivity, finally, I reflect upon the way in which tragic fate serves as a necessary structural component of the story, a backdrop against which both subject and truth are staged.

The action in *O poeta e a inquisição* centers upon Antônio José, the protagonist and tragic hero, and Mariana, an actress who, it is implied, has an amorous relationship with the crypto-Jewish playwright. (In this sense, Magalhães departs from the more biographical approach of Santareno and Azulay, who creatively reproduce his historical marriage to Leonor, as we will see below.) Lúcia, Mariana's maid, and Frei Gil, the perverse priest whose confession I analyze in chapter 3, serve as the secondary characters who complete the dynamic of persecution and martyrdom imposed by the Inquisition.

A melodramatic tone pervades the romantic play, which relies on overdetermined oppositions between heat and cold, day and night, light and dark. The protagonists are depicted as suffering from fevers, oscillating between sweat and chills: Lúcia shrieks in response to Mariana's fever ("Oh, como queima!/Parece um forno! . . . Que terrível febre!" ["Oh, how it burns!/Like an oven! . . . What a terrible fever!"]) (Gonçalves de Magalhães, *O poeta e a inquisição*, 1), while Antônio José wakes up from a nightmare in a cold sweat (16), and Mariana's hands turn to "ice" after being attacked by the corrupt Frei Gil (47). Mariana's anxiety surrounding Antônio José's fate is projected onto the dark night: "Que noite escura! O céu como está negro!/Oh! que noite de horror! . . . nem uma estrela!" ("What a dark night! How dark the sky is!/Oh! What a night of horror! . . . not a single star!") (14). For his part, Antônio José likens his destiny to a day that has ended, taken over by darkness and death: "para mim fechou-se o mundo, e o dia . . ./Para o mundo morri . . . Minha existência/Já não conto por dias; sim por dores!/Nesta perpétua noite sepultado,/É meu único sol esta candeia/Pálida e triste como a luz dos mortos" ("for me the world, and the day, are done/For the world I died . . . My existence/I no longer count by days, but by agonies!/In this perpetual night,/This candle is my only sun/Pale and sad like the light of the dead") (51).

Affect, rather than ideas, dominates the work: Antônio José shouts and cries to Mariana about being pursued while Mariana naively asks who is after him:

> *Antônio José:* . . . Queres pois que mil vezes te repita,
> Que não posso escapar, que me perseguem?
>
> *Mariana:* Mas quem?

Antônio José (com furor): A Inquisição! A inquisição!

Mariana: Oh Deus! A inquisição? (*cheia de horror*)

Antônio José (rindo-se de cólera): O Santo-Ofício!

Mariana: Que horror! A Inquisição! (Gonçalves de Magalhães, *O poeta e a inquisição,* 11)

Antônio José: . . . Do you want me to repeat it one thousand times, That I cannot escape, that they pursue me?

Mariana: But who?

Antônio José (with fury): The Inquisition! The Inquisition!

Mariana: Oh God! The Inquisition? (*full of horror*)

Antônio José (laughing with cholera): The Holy Office!

Mariana: What horror! The Inquisition!

The above lines that, to a contemporary reader, may seem exaggerated or parodic, conform to the romantic norms of the epoch. The excessive repetition of the characters' exclamations of "The Inquisition!" together with the stage directions calling for fury, horror, and cholera, create a dramatic scene in which emotion, together with the looming death that haunts tragedy, suspends agency. The tragic quality of the protagonists finds its ultimate expression in the idea of crypto-Jewishness. As I will detail in chapter 3, the crypto-Jewish subject is always already a guilty subject, at once embodying and subverting the modern idea of the autonomous subject. In her book *Seductions of Fate,* Gabriela Basterra reminds us that the constitution of the modern subject is premised upon guilt, and therefore reproduces the structure of classical tragic subjectivity: "There is a direct correlation between becoming a subject, assuming guilt and depicting oneself as victim. Guilt is therefore the last thing tragic subjects (both classical and modern) would be willing to renounce" (8).

A metatheatrical work about a playwright and an actress, *O poeta e a inquisição* reflects upon the staging of identity from the outset. The opening scene's stage directions specify that Mariana is "sentada, com um papel na mão, como que estuda sua parte teatral" ("seated, with a paper in her hand, as if studying a theatrical role") (1). It turns out that she is, in fact, preparing for the performance of *Ignez de Castro,* a tragedy like *O poeta e a inquisição.* Mariana's role as the eponymous tragic heroine in the play within a play suggests that Gonçalves de Magalhães is interested in contemplating, in addition to the genre of theater, the performative aspect of identity that is central to crypto-Judaism—or, conversely, that he is interested in crypto-Judaism insofar as it reveals a certain aspect of theater, in particular, romantic theater, as we shall see. That Mariana is instructed to read "as if" preparing for a theatrical role implies a tentative or hypothetical quality inherent to performance, a shadow or trace of another possible interpretation.

Yet the articulation of *marranismo* through performance—or of performance through *marranismo*—does not resemble the deconstructive *marranismo* of Berman's *En el nombre de Dios*. In *O poeta e a inquisição*, the ostensibly slippery quality of identity in the opening scene gives way to a more fixed notion of truth as the plot unfolds (linked, for example, to the overdetermined oppositions between heat and cold, day and night). We learn that Antônio José is being pursued by the Inquisitorial authorities not, as Azulay's film will imply, because of the subversive lines in his satirical puppet operas, but because he is accused of Judaizing. Gonçalves de Magalhães's play does not subvert the logic of the Inquisition (even as it announces its transgressions), but rather corroborates its narratives. The church may be portrayed as straying from its principles in pursuing a good man, but the motive for Antônio José's arrest and subsequent martyrdom is based upon something represented as *true:* the Inquisition's stated objective of rooting out heresy among its subjects is never called into question. Although the play casts Inquisitional persecution as transgressive, it nonetheless represents these events as an accurate portrayal of the history of Inquisitorial investigation into heresy in Portugal. *O poeta e a inquisição*, while avoiding the disruption of the ethical, seeks instead to moralize, thus reproducing the logic of the Inquisition.

The motif of hiddenness pervades the work, and is repeated in a number of scenes. As the protagonist hides from the authorities, he must use a disguise, just as actors don costumes for the play within a play. The cloak is provided to him by the Count of Ericeira's servant, and arrives in a locked box. The existence of the box containing a disguise to protect Antônio José, who in turn guards his own secret, suggests a countless number of layers to the protagonist's identity, the "essence" of which is represented as infinitely postponed (in contrast to Ripstein's marrano characters who, deep down, are revealed to be Jewish). At the heart of this layered existence lies, according to the melancholy playwright, a vast mystery, a divine abyss:

> *Antônio José (pensando)*: Há dias aziagos, em que o homem,
> Em profunda tristeza mergulhado,

Se esquece de si mesmo, e se concentra
No mundo interior da consciência,
Nesse abismo mais vasto do que o mundo,
Nesse mistério oculto, indefinível,
Nessa imagem de Deus em nós contida,
Que relata o passado, e ama o futuro. (Gonçalves de Magalhães, *O poeta e a inquisição,* 17–18)

There are sinister days in which man,
Drowning in profound sadness,
Forgets himself, and is lost
In the interior world of consciousness,
In that abyss that is vaster than the world,
In that occult, undefinable mystery
In that image of God contained within us,
That relays the past, and loves the future.

The above passage conveys a notion of interiority that enjoys a place of particular prominence in romanticism in general, and in romantic theater in particular. Here, the idea of an inner world (a privileged locus of enunciation for the artist) grounds itself in the crypto-Jew, a figure whose status as guardian of a secret stands as its defining characteristic.

The depiction of Antônio José's Jewishness, therefore, belongs to a much larger concern with interiority and subjectivity. While the playwright is not shown observing Jewish rites clandestinely (as are the crypto-Jewish Carvajals by both Ripstein and Berman), his "soul" is deemed Jewish by the play. Mariana describes her friend as innocent: "Ele dorme, tão perto da desgraça! / Ele dorme; sua alma é inocente, / Seu coração é puro.—Ai, pobre Antônio!" ("He sleeps, so near disgrace / He sleeps; his soul is innocent, / His heart is pure—Oh, poor Antônio!") (Gonçalves de Magalhães, *O poeta e a inquisição,* 13)—but he guards within him a private truth, confessed later in the play by the protagonist himself as he rages against the injustice of his arrest:

. . . E por que causa?
Por uma opinião, por uma idéia
Que minha mãe herdou de seus maiores,
E a transmitiu ao filho!—E sou culpado! . . .
. . .
Por uma idéia oculta de minha alma?

Por que em vez de seguir a lei de Cristo,
Sigo a Lei de Moysés!. . . (Gonçalves de Magalhães, O *poeta e a*
    inquisição, 52)

And for what reason?
For an opinion, for an idea
That my mother inherited from her elders,
And transmitted to her son!—I am accused! . . .
    . . .
For a hidden idea in my soul?
Because instead of following the law of Christ,
I follow the Law of Moses! . . .

Jewishness, here, is depicted not as a tangible characteristic (he does not behave as a Jew in public or private), but as an inner essence, a "hidden idea." The notion that Antônio José's Jewishness is unavailable to the outside world, an abstract idea rather than a practice, is suggestive of a decidedly modern conception of identity as reflexive self-presence (and, more broadly, of truth). But if we are to read the *ideia oculta* together with the more Derridean notion of the secret as exceeding the play of hiding and revelation, perhaps we can understand modern subjectivity as caught between two logics: that of truth as *alêtheia,* and that of unreadability, rupture, singularity, inassimilability. The rendering of alterity as inaccessible posits interiority as a privileged site of truth and, at the same time, guarantees its threatening quality. That is, rather than emphasizing the performative, destabilizing potential of *marranismo,* the play opts to put forward a more essentialist version of identity in order to avoid the traumatic alternative. Insofar as it is hidden, the existence of Antônio José's Jewishness is preserved, even as it ultimately leads to his demise because, as Basterra argues, "dying is not possible in the tragic universe *as long as one refuses to leave that universe.* As long as death is still part of the tragic universe, as long as one cannot envisage a way of dying *to* the tragic universe, one cannot die" (*Seductions of Fate,* 47). Antônio José's Jewishness is conserved not *despite* his death but *because* of it: tragic fate guarantees the preservation of meaning that it ostensibly destroys. The execution of converts, in this sense, reenacts the primary act of conversion as it aims to remove any and every element of Jewish alterity, even as it is revealed to be an impossible task.

Interestingly, despite Antônio's confession that he follows the Law of Moses, he is never shown actually observing this law, whether in belief or practice. Perhaps it would be more accurate to say, conversely, that the Law of Moses follows him: that, as Derrida has suggested, the marrano does not keep a secret, but rather the secret keeps the marrano. It could be argued, then, that even as the play strives to create a subject whose identity is based upon essentialist notions of Judaism and Christianity, a trace of *something else* remains that resists such a reading (in very much the same way that an inassimilable remainder undermines every effort to convert the Jewish other). Yet it is only in the reading of such theatrical scenes that an opening is created in which it is possible to take into account the constitutive impossibility of conversion (and the impossibility of identity more broadly). In the works that follow, I will continue to interrogate the tension between conversion and resistance, identity and anti-identity, that haunts Antônio José's *marranismo* as well as the narratives that seek to represent it.

Bernardo Santareno's O Judeu

O Judeu, written by Bernardo Santareno (pseudonym of António Martinho do Rosário, among the foremost Portuguese playwrights of the twentieth century), is a 1966 drama that forms part of a larger tradition of politicized allegorizations of the crypto-Jew penned under dictatorship.[29] Called a "dramatic narrative," the nearly 250-page work was not performed until after the death of its author. While I will focus in more detail upon the function of allegory in the following chapter, here I want to investigate the way in which Santareno's version of da Silva offers a distinct reading of the playwright, as well as of *marranismo* more broadly. In particular, I am interested in the way in which Santareno's *Judeu* is secular, atheist, and decidedly *not* Jewish, so that *marranismo* is displaced onto a sort of discursive dialogism that manifests itself in the Protestant (also "converted") narrator, the writer Francisco Xavier de Oliveira.

The António José[30] to whom we are introduced in Santareno's *O Judeu* is virtually unrecognizable if we are to compare him to Gonçalves de Magalhães's tortured leading man: he is, at best, a distant relative. If affect dominates *O poeta e a inquisição*, words and ideas govern the pages of Santareno's *narrativa dramática*: those of da Silva, as well as those of the verbose, narcissistic narrator. While both protagonists could be defined loosely as tragic heroes, Santareno—writing not within the aesthetic context of nineteenth-century Brazilian romanticism but within the political landscape of the Salazar dictatorship in late twentieth-century Portugal—fashions a character out of the historical figure that draws upon the satirical, subversive lines of da Silva's puppet operas while stripping him of any cultural or religious allegiances to Jewishness or Judaism in order to make him readable to a secular, intellectual public.

The play opens during an auto-da-fé (the Inquisitional ritual whereby accused heretics were executed before the masses in the public square), as an Inquisitor delivers a speech to the audience. The audience, for its part, is situated physically in relation to the stage as if witnessing the public spectacle; the stage directions specify that the "[os] espectadores ... funcionam como assistentes do auto-de-fé" ("the spectators serve as onlookers to the auto-da-fé") (Santareno, O *Judeu*, 14). The Padre Pregador's eleven-page monologue—interrupted only briefly by the "popular" voice of an anti-Semitic observer and then again by the resistant voice of the Jewish prisoner—articulates not only the radical anti-Semitism of the Inquisition but retroactively anticipates the reactionary rhetoric of twentieth-century Nazism. While I will address the allegorical impulse of O *Judeu* in chapter 2, I would like to concentrate here upon the Inquisitional logic employed by Santareno: a logic that, counterintuitively, is left virtually unscathed in the politically progressive play. In this opening monologue, Jews and conversos are virtually indistinguishable insofar as they both embody a pathological force in society: the priest compares Jewish heresy to a "leprosy of the soul" and crypto-Jews to vermin—"Como os ratos correm ao queijo, eles vão de desgraça em desgraça, de miséria em miséria: Enganam, corrompem, roubam" ("Like rats flock to cheese, they go from disgrace to disgrace, from misery to misery: They deceive, corrupt, steal") (16). Without elaborating here upon the markedly twentieth-century quality of the rhetoric (Nazi propaganda often likened Jews to vermin), I want to underscore the equivalence established between Jews and New Christians in Inquisitional discourse. According to the Inquisitor, the New Christian can be one of two things: either he is a "pure" Christian welcomed with opened arms by the church (but whose existence is presented as dubious), or a heretic in disguise: "A máscara 'cristão-novo' esconde um judeu velho, um herege relapso, hipócrita, diminuto e obstinado" ("The 'crypto-Jewish' mask hides an old Jew, a relapsed heretic, hypocritical, minute and obstinate") (16). The two voices that momentarily disrupt the inflammatory speech serve to uphold its rationale: on the one hand, an anti-Semitic voice of the common people calling for the death of Jews and, on the other, a Jew who characterizes the religion of his Catholic tormentors as false messianism: "O cristianismo é falso! E falso o seu messias, Jesus Cristo!!!!" ("Christianity is false! And its messiah, Jesus Christ, is false!!!!") (19). Both voices, rather than subverting the logic of the Inquisition—the absolute opposition between Judaism and Christianity, the Schmittian divide between friend and enemy that conditions all politics—guarantee its status as dominant paradigm in the context of the play. That is, even as it is deemed morally wrong, Inquisitional logic remains intact in the dramatic narrative.

Like Gonçalves de Magalhães's Antônio José, Santareno's protagonist suffers the wrath of the Inquisition, blaming his inherited Jewishness (which he himself disavows) for his misfortune. Rather than assuming Judaism as his own, he instead projects it onto his mother, who stands metonymically for the whole of his plagued heritage: "todo o meu mal vem de a senhora ser minha mãe: Judia! Judia, judia!" ("all of my malady comes from you being my mother: Jew! Jew, Jew!") (Santareno, *O Judeu*, 50), and later, "Porque me deixou nascer? A mãe sabia . . . sabia muito bem o que a vida tinha para me dar. Cão judeu . . . leproso . . . porco! Judeu, judeu, judeu! . . ." ("Why did she bring me into this world? My mother knew . . . she knew perfectly well what life had in store for me. Jewish dog . . . leper . . . pig! Jew, Jew, Jew! . . .") (56). Antônio José rages against his tainted legacy, rejecting Jewish beliefs and practices in favor of an atheism that would liberate him from his suffering: "Não acredito, não creio em nada disso! Quero viver!! Não creio no Deus de Israel, não creio no Deus dos cristãos . . . Tenho medo de todos os deuses, messias, profetas e santos. Medo!" ("I don't believe, I don't believe in any of this! I want to live!! I don't believe in the God of Israel, I don't believe in the God of the Christians . . . I am afraid of all of the gods, messiahs, prophets and saints. Afraid!") (57). The protagonist's atheism firmly places him within the camp of the twentieth-century secular intellectual left, Santareno's ideal public.

As much as Santareno's Antônio José may, on the surface, remind the reader of Gonçalves de Magalhães's tempestuous protagonist, the narrator Cavaleiro de Oliveira explains that rather than remaining a slave to his emotion, the tormented artist converts his anguish into art:

> António José achou um mar, largo e fundo, para desaguar o rio dos seus tormentos e medos: Escreve! Que escreverá ele? Versos . . . Conversas para os bonifrates? . . . Achaste, meu rapaz! . . . Escreve com a mesma fúria de paixão com que um qualquer mortal se ceva na mulher amada. Encontrou-

se; António José da Silva encontrou-se com o mais remoto, profundo e autêntico dos seus rostos: o da poesia dramática. . . . O sangue faz-se verbo. E o verbo ressurreição. (Santareno, *O Judeu*, 96–97)

António José discovered a sea, long and deep, into which the river of his torments and fears could flow: He writes! What will he write? Verses . . . Triflings for fools? . . . You guessed it, my friend! . . . He writes with the same fury and passion with which any mortal is nourished by the woman he loves. He found himself; António José da Silva found himself in the most remote, profound and authentic of his faces: that of dramatic poetry. . . . Blood made verb. And the verb resurrection.

That the above description of António's conversion of fury into poetry is made with recourse to a markedly Christian rhetoric (blood made verb, verb resurrection) is significant. Here, conversion is both thematized and performed: describing the conversion of the playwright's passion into art, the narrative subject himself realizes a conversion of Jew into Christian, as though it were necessary for the modern playwright to *reconvert* the converso.

Despite the Christ-centered language in which the protagonist's transformation into artist is conveyed, he is nonetheless presented as an atheist and humanist, as I claim above. António José again insists upon his godlessness in a later argument with his cousin (and now wife) Leonor:

Leonor (lucidez cansada): Tu e eu somos o que eles marcaram que fôssemos *(com violência)*: Tu és judeu. Eu sou judia.

António José: Eu sou tão-só um homem. Nem mais, nem menos. Nem raro espírito, nem singular de corpo. Um homem; um qualquer. Tu, uma mulher sem marcas; uma no meio das gentes. Esta é a verdade *(violento, agressivo)*: A verdade!!

Leonor (num grito): Não a deles! Judeu, judeu, judeu . . . ! *(Esconde a cabeça no corpo da filha, em soluços.)*

António José (obstinado): Nem judeu, nem cristão. Um homem sem fé. Sem deuses. (147)

Leonor (with tired clarity): You and I are what they say we are *(violently)*: You are a Jew. I am a Jew.

> *António José:* I am just a man. No more, no less. Neither rare in spirit, nor singular in body. A man; any man. You, a woman without marks; one in the midst of a crowd. This is the truth (*violent, aggressive*): The truth!!
>
> *Leonor (yelling):* Not their truth! Jew, Jew, Jew . . . ! (*She hides her head in her daughter's body, sobbing.*)
>
> *António José (obstinate):* Neither a Jew, nor a Christian. A man without faith. Without gods.

The confrontation between husband and wife is significant in its embodiment of one of the principal conflicts of the marrano (and later of the secular, assimilated Jew in western Europe): while Leonor insists upon the official identitary classifications maintained by Inquisition authorities, the poet aspires to the modern, humanist model of the universal sovereign subject, unblemished by differentiating traits. I want to suggest, however, that these competing logics, while ostensibly opposed, are actually quite intimately related, and that it is the marrano—conflicted, divided, at once same and other—that calls both models into question. This latter possibility is not allowed for in Santareno, however: the politics of 1966, of Portugal under a repressive regime, calls for another form of resistance, one in which right and wrong are situated at opposite ends of a moral pole, in which the subversion of these poles is feared to render political resistance useless.

It is therefore the narrator himself, also a convert, who stands as the only feasible voice of authority within the dramatic work. That the Cavaleiro de Oliveira has converted from Catholicism to Protestantism, rather than Judaism to Catholicism, is important for two principal reasons. First, the contemporary spectator of Santareno's play is less likely to view a Protestant as a heretic, despite the survival of Catholicism as the dominant religion in Portugal. Second, the Cavaleiro narrates from outside the nation, from the privileged position of exile in London, the ostensibly culturally superior site of twentieth-century Europe, the locus of reason and democracy that has eluded the Iberian country on the margins of twentieth-century European democratic modernity. If *O Judeu* is represented as an inescapably Jewish (and thus inevitably tragic) figure, it is the Cavaleiro de Oliveira that stands as the successful convert, marginalizing Jewishness in favor of an intellectual voice through which it becomes possible to denounce twentieth-century totalitarianism.

Jom Tob Azulay's O Judeu

Written and filmed in the mid-1980s, Azulay's *O Judeu* (which finally made its debut in 1996) does not respond directly to totalitarian violence, as does Santareno's, but rather emerges during a period in which the transition from dictatorship to democracy, and a new, subtler, more decentered violence begins to characterize Brazilian culture. The plot, which commences during Antônio José's childhood, chronicles the period between the two arrests of the playwright by the Inquisition, the second of which culminates in an auto-da-fé in which he is publicly burned at the stake. In Azulay's film, violence and crypto-subjectivity are codified through the visual: specifically, through the tension between *spectacle* and *spectrality.* I want to suggest here that Azulay's film moves beyond Magalhães's and Santareno's representations of da Silva in its conjugation of visibility and secrecy to deconstruct not only New Christian but Old Christian identity as well. In this sense, Azulay does not reproduce Inquisitional logic (as does Santareno, even as he attempts to subvert it), but rather exposes a chasm at the heart of the modern subject, a subject that is always already a crypto-subject. I will conclude the discussion by suggesting—in dialogue with Heinrich von Kleist's "Über das Marionettentheater" and Paul de Man's reading of Kleist—that performance understood broadly, and marionette theater in particular, offers Azulay a productive medium through which to deconstruct the crypto-subject.[31]

The notion of spectrality has been taken up by Derrida in his 1994 *Specters of Marx* as the haunting presence of a foreign body within the same. Proposing the neologism "hauntology," he plays with the tension between haunting and being: in French, of course, *hantologie* is aurally indistinguishable from *ontologie,* so that the silent "h" haunts ontology, just as the specter haunts being. This aporetic relationship between that which is hidden and that which is revealed, the "secret" and the "seen," is relevant to our discussion not only because we are talking about a visual genre—film—but also because, as I have discussed, one of the principal motifs that has been used to characterize crypto-Jewish identity is the idea of masking or masquerade. While in the following chapter I will detail the ethico-political demand posed by Inquisition allegories as spectral ruins, here I want to underscore the undecidable relation between secrecy and revelation in Azulay's film.

Since da Silva came from a family of crypto-Jews who continued to practice their religion clandestinely, the film, which takes as its point of departure the period following the family's arrest in Rio de Janeiro and trial in Lisbon, emphasizes the idea of performance from the very first scene, in which a young Antônio and his cousins put on a play for the adults. Before a public of relatives and friends, the children stage a drama of their own creation, an amateur skit that culminates in the scapegoating of one character, whom the others target as a crypto-Jew. In a climactic scene, two characters accuse a third of being a Jewish convert, shouting the epithet "*Cristão novo! Cristão novo!* . . . Morte ao *cristão novo!*" ("Marrano! Marrano! . . . Death to the marrano!"). The children, unaware of their own family's clandestine religious loyalties, reproduce the anti-Semitic rhetoric they've heard on the streets of Rio de Janeiro. After the play, Antônio's mother takes the children aside to confess the "truth" of the family's identity, a moment the film represents as initiating the playwright's inner torment: that night, Antônio tells his siblings, "Não vou conseguir dormir nunca mais" ("I won't be able to sleep ever again").

If the children's play echoes the dominant discourse of the time, Antônio's later work—a product not only of his anguish as a marrano, but also of his traumatic experience of imprisonment and torture by the Inquisition—occupies the realm of doubt and subversion. The creator of what came to be known as "puppet opera," da Silva designed elaborate marionettes to interpret roles in comedies that parodied the dominant political, social, and religious ideas of the era (such as justice, marriage, and heaven).[32] His plays and puppet operas not only entertained a vast public in Lisbon's Bairro Alto, they titillated the Portuguese elite who felt themselves to be culturally behind the rest of Europe, and provoked anxiety in the reactionary Santo Ofício. The main chronological trajectory of the film, which details the events of Antônio's life in Lisbon, is interspersed with scenes from his puppet operas: lively, irreverent clips that hint at the motivation behind the Inquisition's persecution of the playwright. Through the lines of the seemingly harmless puppets, the Lisbon public is exposed to witty dialogue that strikes at the heart of the power structures in place at the time, to a discourse that could not have been voiced directly.

After assembling his first marionette, Antônio uses the puppet to invite Leonor, his then-future wife, on their first date. Antônio arrives at her home as she is lighting Sabbath candles in the closet, a practice common among crypto-Jews. Leonor and her servant do not comment upon the clandestine ritual, so that the viewer who is unfamiliar with crypto-Judaic practice can only begin to guess at what precisely is being hidden by the women. Midway through the surreptitious rite, Leonor is surprised by a knock on the door; outside, Antônio's puppet is waiting with a poem prepared to seduce her. The secretive, flirtatious courtship draws on the dynamic of hiding reminiscent of Cyrano de Bergerac, in which ventriloquism and poetry come together to cultivate desire. By creating a double masquerade, in which Leonor practices a "closeted" Judaism while Antônio hides behind his marionette, Azulay underscores the performative—and seductive—quality of marrano subjectivity.

If Azulay draws upon the conventional notion that the crypto-Jew must fashion a public mask in order to conceal her "authentic" identity—a limited metaphor in its implication of a "true" essence beneath a "false" projection—he begins to deconstruct this model by suggesting that the church and crown, too, employ theatrics in order to perform power. In a scene immediately following one of da Silva's operatic productions, Dom João V is shown making a grand entrance, surrounded by his court, dressed in full "costume" and walking in a choreographed sway to his throne. The church, too, taps into the power of the spectacle through the horrific display of victims in the auto-da-fé. By portraying New Christians as well as religious and secular authorities as costumed actors, Azulay exposes the way in which identities are imagined and performed across social, political, and religious lines. This rhetorical strategy recalls Judith Butler's analysis of gender performativity in *Gender Trouble:* the drag queen destabilizes normative ideas about gender not simply by embodying a transgressive form of femininity, but rather because by performing femininity, she exposes all gender identity as performance (146, 338).[33] But since the performance of power also enables or enacts power (not only in the context of the baroque, though it takes on a very specific form in this context), it is only through Azulay's juxtaposition of puppetry and posing on *both* sides of the power divide that it becomes possible to read the entire social milieu of early-eighteenth-century Lisbon, and not just the world of the crypto-Jew, as a staging of identity and subjectivity.

The other side of this highly visual and visible culture is that what is secret or absent from the stage is equally, if not more powerfully, present. As I have argued, it is the unreadability of the converted Jew, the fact that the marrano secret is *neither* locked in a crypt *nor* confessable, that provokes anxiety and reactionary violence in the Old Christian subject. This is perhaps most evident in the discourse of interrogation, in which a confession—the acknowledgment of identifiable difference—merits a lighter sentence than denial. Antônio's cousin Brites, the only character to explicitly defend Judaism and attack Christianity before her confessor, is pronounced insane, freeing her from the pain of torture and death. Once again, however, the dynamic of secrecy and revelation, visibility and invisibility, does not solely belong to the domain of the New Christian: the very foundation of the Inquisition is portrayed by the film as one of concealment and deceit. When Antônio's confessor, suspecting that his prisoner has not in fact been denounced by anyone and has, therefore, been illegally apprehended, approaches the General Inquisitor in order to express his concern, Dom Nuno chastises his subordinate for succumbing to reason over faith: "Séculos da sabedoria do Santo Ofício não se revela em meia hora de buscas furtivas. Eu próprio não me atreveria a dizer que conheço todas as regras. . . . A sabedoria maior vem nas entrelinhas" ("Centuries of the wisdom of the Inquisition are not revealed in a furtive half-hour search. I myself would not dare to say that I know all the rules. . . . the greatest wisdom can be read between the lines"). The inaccessibility of the Law—reminiscent of Kafka's parable "Before the Law," to which we shall return in chapter 3—evokes the notion of a void at the heart of the Holy Office, an empty space around which unreadable rules and unquestionable power are structured. The infinite postponement of comprehension of the Law in Dom Nuno's insistence that the greatest knowledge resides between the lines exposes the fictional—yet very real—nature of the church's power, again, no less a performance than the converso's projected faith.

That the church's power resides in the interpretation of the Law, that reading "between the lines" can yield the greatest insight into Inquisitorial violence, that it is within the scene of reading, finally, in which the key to both domination and resistance can be found, prove crucial to understanding not only da Silva's use of marionettes, but also Azulay's incorporation of puppetry into the genre of film. In conclusion, then, I turn to Heinrich von Kleist's "Über das Marionettentheater" ("On the Marionette Theatre"), which relates the conversation of two men—the narrator and a friend, the principal dancer at a local theater—on art, beauty, and mimesis. The narrator describes to the dancer the impression made upon him by the marionette show he'd had the opportunity to observe in the marketplace, and inquires about the relationship between the marionette and its operator, wondering if the latter must embody the sensibilities of a dancer in order to make his puppet move with grace and verisimilitude. The dancer responds that the marionette, by moving around a center of gravity, not only approximates the movements of a dancer, but can—in principle—surpass the dancer's grace because "it would never be guilty of affectation." This explanation strikes a chord in the narrator, who responds with a second example of how "consciousness can disturb grace":

> "I was at the baths with a young man who was then remarkably graceful. He was about fifteen, and only faintly could one see the first traces of vanity, a product of the favours shown him by women. It happened that we had recently seen in Paris the figure of the boy pulling a thorn out of his foot. The cast of the statue is well known; you see it in most German collections. My friend looked into a tall mirror just as he was lifting his foot to a stool to dry it, and he was reminded of the statue. He smiled and told me of his discovery. As a matter of fact, I'd noticed it too, at the same moment, but . . . I don't know if it was to test the quality of his apparent grace or to provide a salutary counter to his vanity . . . I laughed and said he must be imagining things. He blushed. He lifted his foot a second time, to show me, but the effort was a failure, as anybody could have foreseen. He tried it again a third time, a fourth time, he must have lifted his foot ten times, but it was in vain. He was quite unable to reproduce the same movement."

In this scene, the problem of mimesis takes center stage. The inability of the youth to reproduce his own gesture, of a mere human to mimic ideal beauty, strips aesthetic mimesis of its power while preserving the notion of the ideal original. In both examples, perfection is attainable, but only in aesthetic objects.

In "Aesthetic Formalization: Kleist's *Über das Marionettentheater*," de Man dwells upon the productive gap between the puppet and its operator, on the one hand, and the puppet and the dancer, on the other. De Man reads Kleist's piece as enacting an "unsettling of mimesis," in which original and copy are deconstructed in the moment of storytelling through the alteration between direct quotation and *style indirect libre,* as well as in the scene of reading itself ("Aesthetic Formalization," 274). According to de Man, "the technique of imitation becomes the hermeneutics of signification," drawing attention away from "actual meaning" and redirecting it to "the process of signification" (281). This is why the ostensibly central problem of Kleist's piece turns out to be a decoy, a distraction from the "true" problem: the impossibility of mimesis, the instability of original and copy, and the recentering of the question of meaning onto the process of signification, or reading. The fact that the imitated statue is of a body in pain (a boy removing a thorn from his foot) suggests that even the "original" pose exhibits a blemished quality.

De Man is careful to point out that the relationship between original and copy is always situated in a triangular relationship with a figure of authority (art critic, Inquisitor, etc.), so that it is the *representation* or reading of this pose that assumes importance. "Maybe the delusion was to believe that the model was graceful in the first place," de Man suggests, asking "is it not the point of aesthetic form that imitates a work of art (ek-phrasis) to substitute the spectacle of pain for the pain itself, and thus sublimate it by drawing away from the pains of experience, focusing instead on the pleasures of imitation?" ("Aesthetic Formalization," 278, 280). De Man's glossing of Kleist sheds light upon a crucial aspect of puppetry and performance: beyond masquerade, the marionette does not destabilize the idea of the mimetic through its own success or failure. Rather, its failure can only be addressed through a fictional narration of the problem, through a figurative re-codification and its subsequent reading.

The exposure of the impossibility of mimesis in Azulay's film through the notion of marrano as marionette does not only read crypto-Jewish identity as performative, but understands identity in general as a performance or creative projection, rather than the expression of an interior essence. The idea that masquerade does not disguise a hidden, positive identity but rather creatively fashions an original projection of subjectivity brings us back to Forster's claim that the marrano represents a fissure at the heart of the modern subject, so that we can read modern subjectivity, together with Derrida, as a universalization of the marrano: the modern subject is always already a crypto-subject. What is hidden from view is not transgressive Jewishness, but rather the traumatic kernel that stands at the center of both New Christian and Old, the troubling fact that our identitary projections orbit around an unsuturable gap between signifier and signified.

Yet, as we learn not only from historical perceptions of New Christians but also in the modern aesthetic works that thematize them, a stubborn desire for positive proof of essence (essential sameness, essential difference) persists. This is why in each of the works discussed in this chapter—from Ripstein's and Berman's portrayals of the Carvajals to Magalhães's, Santareno's, and Azulay's rendering of da Silva—there exists an explicit tension between an insistence upon hidden Jewishness, on the one hand, and a refusal of or resistance to this idea, whether through the meta-performances of Holy Week in Berman or da Silva's puppet theater in Azulay. The idea of Jewishness as "uma ideia oculta" put forth by Magalhães, while rooted in a decidedly romantic notion of subjectivity and truth, speaks to an anxiety surrounding crypto-Jewishness and identity that permeates the Luso-Hispanic cultural imaginary from the fourteenth century to the present day. Derrida's notion of hauntology—the idea that the specters of history return to the present in order to pose an ethico-political demand—is therefore crucial to our understanding of modern Inquisition narratives, which repeatedly negotiate the boundary between secrecy and exposure. In the following chapter, I unpack the relationship between historical allegory, ruins, and haunting, asking why it is that these tales are most effectively told through allegory as mode of signification.

CHAPTER 2

Allegory and Hauntology

Ghosts, like . . . allegories, are manifestations from the realm
of mourning; they have an affinity for mourners, for those
who ponder over signs and over the future.
—Walter Benjamin

Allegories are always allegories of metaphor and, as such,
they are always allegories of the impossibility of reading.
—Paul de Man

In the spring of 2002—mere months after watching the Twin Towers fall
and dust-covered, distressed financial district workers hastily migrate
uptown past the Greenwich Village campus buildings of New York University, where I was a graduate student at the time—I attended a Broadway production of Arthur Miller's *The Crucible*. Starring Liam Neeson
and Laura Linney as John and Elizabeth Proctor, the play was at once a
welcome escape from the distressed atmosphere of the city streets outside of the theater, and an uncomfortable reminder that Americans were
still, more than 300 years after the Salem Witch Trials dramatized by
Miller, imagining and hunting down enemies both domestic and foreign.
The war in Afghanistan was well under way, and then-President George
W. Bush was making regular televised speeches to his constituents on
the axis of evil and other such paranoid, bellicose constructs.

Yet as I sat in the theater, I couldn't help but feel that Miller's use
of the Salem story in order to express a thinly veiled criticism of the
anti-communist fervor of the 1950s amounted to a violent appropria-
tion of history. While the depiction of witch-hunting in early colonial
New England certainly provided an apt setting within which to ponder questions of scapegoating and blacklisting, desire and guilt, power
and politics in the mid-twentieth century, I couldn't rid myself of the

thought that Miller's aesthetic leap into the past in order to address the present—however potent—did so at the expense of the historical specificity of the seventeenth-century witch hunts, the singularity of Salem. I detected in the use of historical allegory a sort of discursive violence, in which the thematization of the past turned event into object.

It therefore took me rather by surprise when, midway through act 3—in which the protagonist, John Proctor, appears in court to defend his wife and neighbors against the false charges of witchcraft—Judge Danforth uttered the following lines: "a person is either with this court or he must be counted against it, there be no road between" (Miller, *The Crucible*, 87). At that point, an audible gasp could be heard from the audience, who could not help but hear in Danforth's accusation President Bush's November 2001 proclamation that "you're either with us or against us in the fight against terror." I realized at that moment—in which the words of a mid-twentieth-century theatrical work that took as its subject matter the religious politics of seventeenth-century colonial New England unexpectedly, hauntingly *mattered* to a twenty-first-century public—that the foundational period of the United States could erupt (and re-erupt) into the present moment: like a specter.

The present chapter focuses upon the spectral quality of allegory by investigating the way in which the turn to the Inquisition in late-twentieth-century theater and film relies upon the use of historical allegory, which I read as proper to the logic of hauntology. Placing Walter Benjamin's idea of the skull or "death's head" (in *The Origin of German Tragic Drama*) alongside Jacques Derrida's notion of the "specter" (in *Specters of Marx*), I want to locate these Inquisition (hi)stories at the juncture between allegory, ruins, and haunting, arguing that the remains of historical violence disturb the present through the literary. Following an analysis of Miller's play, I turn my attention to three Inquisition allegories: Arturo Ripstein's *El Santo Oficio* (1974) and Sabina Berman's *En el nombre de Dios* (1991), which project contemporary ethnic and class struggles onto a sixteenth-century context, and Bernardo Santareno's *O Judeu* (1966), which links Inquisitorial violence to twentieth-century authoritarianism and genocide.[1] Challenging the assumption, predominant in some critical circles, that allegorical representation, particularly in the context of political repression, serves as a disguise that masks or covers the "real" story (that is, the idea that the "truth" cannot be told for fear of censorship or punishment), I attempt to locate another side of allegory, in which the ruins of history serve as the condition of both possibility and impossibility for contemporary readings of violence and totalitarianism. I claim that allegory functions as a *mode of significa-tion*[2] that exhibits a constitutive aporetic quality, in which the representation of "history" sets the stage for the arrival (from the past as absolute future) of an unexpected event that, through productive anachronism, exposes time as "out of joint."

BENJAMIN'S SKULL MEETS DERRIDA'S SPECTER

While it could be argued that Miller—or Ripstein, or Berman, or Santareno—turns to allegory *precisely in order to haunt* the contemporary viewer, I want to suggest that within each work we encounter, in the act of reading, discursive shards that pierce each performance or interpretation, whether they work for or against what we might imagine to be authorial intention (if such a thing were possible to determine). In his critique of German tragic drama, Benjamin already anticipates the demise of the idea of intentionality, arguing that "allegory emerges from the depths of being to intercept the intention, and to triumph over it" (*Origin of German Tragic Drama*, 183). The 2010 Broadway musical *The Burnt Part Boys*—which depicted the horror of a fictional West Virginia coal mine collapse and fire—debuted just two months after dozens of workers were killed in a mining accident in the same state. The unfortunate timing of the debut could not possibly have been planned, yet it did not make the effect on the viewing public any less powerful. If anything, the *unintentionality* of the production's timing proved that much more disquieting for its unhappy coincidence. In both Broadway productions, as well as in the Inquisition allegories I will read below, I want to suggest that the horror of the uncanny interrupts any attempt to control or impose meaning, whether in the act of writing or in the moment of reading.

The present chapter builds upon my argument in previous work that just as the historical conversion of Jews, which violently assimilated the Jewish other into the imperialism of the same, left *remainders* of Jewish difference, contemporary artistic works that seek to figuratively absorb the other of history into the present are similarly disrupted by an element of alterity that makes total incorporation impossible (Graff Zivin, "Conversiones textuales," 259–61; Graff Zivin, *Wandering Signifier*, 119–25). This traumatic kernel that stands at the heart of the aesthetic work behaves as a specter in the sense discussed by Derrida, a spirit-become-flesh that is neither spirit nor flesh. Reflecting upon the legacy of Marx and Marxism after the fall of communism, Derrida defines the specter (which he confesses to having unconsciously "remembered" from the opening lines of *The Communist Manifesto*) as "a paradoxical incorporation, the becoming-body, a certain phenomenal and carnal form of the spirit . . . some 'thing' that remains difficult to name: neither soul nor body, and both one and the other" (*Specters of Marx*, 5). He understands the specter as something that "no longer belongs to knowledge"; it is "an unnameable or almost unnameable thing" (5). Like the unexpected appearance of the ghost of Hamlet's father in Shakespeare, the specter's reapparition conveys the sense that "the time is out of joint," revealing that something is *not right* about the present, what Derrida denominates the "originary corruption of the day of today" (25). Keeping the dynamic of hauntology in mind, the present chapter poses the following questions: What do these Inquisition narratives come back to tell us? Why do they return, and in what way can their return be understood as an arrival? Can we understand the past from which they travel as "absolute future"? What is the precise relationship between repetition (past) and singularity (future) in these works?[3]

The place of allegory in the Latin American literary tradition—indeed, as fundamental to the very institution of Latin American literature—has been treated by countless critics. Fredric Jameson, Doris Sommer, Alberto Moreiras, Idelber Avelar, and, most recently, Kate Jenckes stand among the myriad scholars that identify in Latin American literary production and criticism a stubborn persistence of the allegorical. After Jameson infamously makes the claim in 1986 that "all Third World texts are . . . national allegories" ("World Literature," 141), Doris Sommer argues for an allegorical reading of nineteenth-century national romances in her 1991 book *Foundational Fictions* (instead of the second-wave feminist slogan "the personal is political," Sommer asserts that the erotic is the national). Her study, while crucial to the understanding of literary practices in the early stages of national independence, risks proposing what Jameson describes as a "one-to-one table of equivalences" in which each figure possesses a corollary in "reality" (Jameson, "World Literature," 146–47). Alberto Moreiras makes a significant critical departure from the idea of national allegory in favor of an approach to Latin American literary and cultural studies that would eschew both identity and difference (seen as opposite sides of the same coin) in *Tercer espacio* (1995) and *The Exhaustion of Difference* (2001). In the spirit of Moreiras's deconstructive criticism, finally, Kate Jenckes employs the idea of allegory as "allography" (derived from the Greek for "other writing"), drawing upon Tom Cohen's neologism in her book *Reading Borges After Benjamin* (2007).[4]

The critical attention to allegory has grown in recent decades, as allegorical works created, published, or produced under dictatorship have drawn interest on both sides of the Atlantic. Southern Cone post-dictatorship literary criticism and Spanish and Portuguese cultural studies have focused upon the way in which writers and artists repeatedly turn to allegory to articulate questions of political resistance, memory, and mourning in the face of authoritarianism. While Spanish literary and cultural studies have paid particular attention to the role of allegory in cinematic representations of the Spanish Civil War and the decades of repressive rule by Franco (Acevedo-Muñoz, Evans, Kinder, Labanyi, Martí-Olivella, Smith), in Portugal we find a number of narrative uses of allegory that respond to the repressive years of the Salazar dictatorship.[5]

But if the allegorical unquestionably enjoys a place of prominence in dictatorship and post-dictatorship literature, readings of such literature—both within and outside of Iberian and Ibero-American literary studies—tend to be rather reductive. Before Idelber Avelar's *The Untimely Present*, which argues for a Benjaminian understanding of the relationship between mourning and allegory in post-dictatorial narrative, allegory has commonly been understood as performing a masking function in the context of totalitarianism. In order to disguise the "true" meaning of the text, such readings suggest, allegory posits a secondary, "false" story: "writers are forced to resort to 'indirect way,' 'metaphors,' and 'allegories' to 'express' what is invariably thought to be a self-identical content that could remain so inside another rhetorical cloak in times of 'free expression'" (Avelar, *Untimely Present*, 9). Such a facile interpretation of the use of allegory relies heavily on an outmoded understanding of, among other things, the idea of authorial intent, the transparency of language, and the link between signifier and signified. Going against this trend, Avelar explains that allegorical narratives predominate in dictatorship and post-dictatorship culture "not because in order to escape censorship writers have to craft 'allegorical' ways of saying things that they would otherwise be able to express 'directly'. . . . but because the petrified images of ruins, in their immanence, bear the only possibility of narrating the defeat" (*Untimely Present*, 69).[6] My reading of Inquisition narratives, in a sense, traverses a path between these two alternatives. While I absolutely depart from the former reading in favor of Avelar's, I want to insist upon the attractiveness of the former and its relevance, precisely because of its desirability, to a discussion about the way in which allegory *works,* that is, the way in which it produces meaning.[7]

To begin with, there is something alluring about the idea of a coded message. Among the factors that make allegory simultaneously unsettling and satisfying is the sense the reader or spectator has of familiarity or recognition of a truth set in *another* time or place: "I am watching a play about the Salem Witch Trials/Inquisition, yet I know it is 'really' about McCarthyism/Francoism/and so on," one is tempted to think. While I maintain that this is a reductive approach to allegory, that the potential meaning(s) of an aesthetic work must dwell in some space beyond the recognizable, I acknowledge the existence of a (tenuous, contingent) relationship of identity between signifier and signified, between witches and communists, marranos and Indians: at the very least because the reader *desires* such a relationship. Yet what makes the experience of identity so potent is precisely the *discontinuity* or rupture between past and present, message and meaning, so that we are speaking of a relationship of interrupted identity, or impossible identity. Allegory gestures toward the self-identical while at the same time imposing a break that makes the reconciliation of singular events unattainable.

Perhaps we can begin to understand the chasm between events as belonging to the order of desire, a dynamic that recalls the phenomenon of *marranismo* detailed in the previous chapter.[8] While the motif of masquerade might seem appealing in the delay or deferral of meaning that it posits—I know that beyond the false projection of "Christianness" lies a hidden, authentic "Jewishness" that nevertheless remains inaccessible to me—this model ultimately proves reductive. More threatening, and therefore more attractive, is the possibility that what lies at the heart of the marrano is an indecipherable secret. Desire, then, appears in response to a demand to read that which is illegible because my fantasy is structured, necessarily, around the irreducible lack in the other. Allegory as hauntology therefore appears both as an inheritance and a call, an unreadable legacy that poses the challenge, "read me, will you ever be able to do so?" (Derrida, *Specters of Marx,* 18). Because, as with marrano identity, it is tempting to characterize allegory as a mask (x) disguising a face (y), *marranismo* as a theme lends itself rather nicely to allegory. If Avelar argues for the idea of an *allegorical crypt* as "the remainder that names the phantasmic persistence of unresolved mourning work" (*Untimely Present,* 8), we can understand allegory as crypto-narrative, and the allegory of crypto-Jews as a double or metacritical allegory: these are stories that operate simultaneously on the levels of (crypto-)form and (crypto-)content. While acknowledging the lure of the mask, then, I will insist upon the remainder as that which determines the rhetorical power of allegory.

Historical allegories—allegorical works that take as their subject a historical event or epoch—pose an even greater challenge for a deconstructive reading in that they appear, at first glance, to restrict rather than broaden possibilities of interpretation. It is amusing to note that Wikipedia's entry on allegory provides an inventory of examples of allegory in art, and argues against the inclusion of *The Crucible* on the list, despite the fact that it has been widely read (one might say overread) as a commentary on McCarthyism. I think, however, that even such narrow approaches to allegory—if unpacked—can lead to potentially fruitful avenues of analysis. The necessarily referential quality of historical allegory, over and above imbuing the text with a certain social or political density, challenges the reader to think beyond the present (or the text's present) and to reread the present from this altered perspective. Historical allegory offers, at least in theory, an *anachronistic* approach to reading, but it is a productive anachronism. To what extent can we argue that historical allegory always already refers to the signified of the present, and to what extent can we locate a limit to this relation of equivalence, a supplement to the textual economy of allegorical signification?

Even when it is not employed within a historical drama, allegory bears a fundamental bond to the historical if we are to follow the work of Walter Benjamin (in *The Origin of German Tragic Drama*) and Paul de Man (in *Allegories of Reading*), who argue that the allegorical (in contrast to the symbolic) necessarily relies upon the element of time. Benjamin, who tries to rescue allegory from its inferior status within art criticism since the romantic tradition, explains (citing Freidrich Creuzer) that the romantics locate in the symbol "momentary totality" while in allegory "we have progression in a series of moments" (*Origin of German Tragic Drama*, 165). In a similar vein, de Man associates the symbol with simultaneity "whereas, in the world of allegory, time is the originary constitutive category" (*Allegories of Reading*, 4).[9] Avelar draws upon this distinction in his discussion of the use of allegory in post-dictatorship literature by referring to perhaps the richest and most oft-quoted passage in Benjamin's essay on *Trauerspiel*: "Whereas in the symbol destruction is idealized and the transfigured face of nature is fleetingly revealed in the light of redemption, in allegory the observer is confronted with the *facies hippocratica* of history as a petrified, primordial landscape. Everything about history that, from the very beginning, has been untimely, sorrowful, unsuccessful, is expressed in a face—or rather in a death's head" (*Origin of German Tragic Drama,* 166). Time as history, and history as a skull or "death's head," are therefore fundamental to any and every use of allegory. Yet it is crucial to clarify that we are speaking of a concept of historicity that exceeds linearity, which is why the anachronistic quality of the specter is vital. Derrida clarifies that haunting is untimely: "historical" but not "*dated*" (*Specters of Marx,* 3). In this sense, the liminal quality of the specter adds a vital dimension to Benjamin's petrified skull, although Benjamin himself seems already to account for the haunting quality of history when he compares allegories to ghosts: "Ghosts, like the profoundly significant allegories, are manifestations from the realm of mourning; they have an affinity for mourners, for those who ponder over signs and over the future" (*Origin of German Tragic Drama,* 193).

The relationship between mourning and allegory is pivotal to Avelar's reading of post-dictatorship literature as sorrowful, an argument that follows the work of Alberto Moreiras, who in *Tercer Espacio* situates post-dictatorial mourning within the Latin American literary tradition of the "lost object." While Inquisition allegories often surface within the historical context of political repression, I want to move in a slightly different direction in my reading, underscoring the haunting quality of allegory. I seek to understand how it is that the specter of the Inquisition "arrives" in the present moment as if from the future precisely in order to expose the corrupt nature of the present. That the appearance of the specter is at once a return (repetition) and an arrival (event), as we shall see in the close readings below, depends upon the referentiality of the historical at the same time that it insists, anachronistically, upon the idea that "the time is out of joint."

CONTEMPORARY CRUCIBLES

Allegorical theater—theater as allegory, and allegory as
theater—never definitively takes place. Not just because
whatever it displays could, qua allegory, mean something
other than what it appears to be, but because the space of the
stage, which it inhabits, is no more definite or stable.
—Samuel Weber

The relationship of referentiality between the Salem Witch Trials and 1950s McCarthyism in Arthur Miller's *The Crucible* has been both downplayed and exaggerated.[10] Program notes to the play's numerous productions tend to inflate the connection between historical events, while Wikipedia insists in its entry on "allegory" that despite the associations between events, *The Crucible* is not an allegorical work. It is difficult to determine whether the latter statement is based upon an overly narrow definition of the rhetorical device (the entry provides a detailed, though hardly comprehensive, list of examples from the genres of narrative, theater, and the visual arts), or if it resists colloquial definitions of the rhetorical tool. For the purpose of my reading, it is sufficient that the play debuted in 1953, during the House Un-American Activities Committee (HUAC) proceedings and the surrounding cultural hysteria to which Miller fell prey (though his own involvement in the congressional hearings did not come until several years later), and—perhaps most importantly—that the play has been *interpreted* as a critique of McCarthyism in particular and "witch hunts" understood more broadly. It is the *context* and *reception* of the play—not Miller's "intention"—that begs such a reading.

Using a vocabulary strikingly similar to Shakespeare's, Miller relates the feeling he had after being convicted of contempt of court and sentenced to prison in 1957, four years after the debut of *The Crucible*, in the following way: "I was just out of sync with the whole country . . . I simply couldn't find a way into the country anymore. . . . I had a sense that the time had gotten away from me" (Miller, *The Crucible*, xxiii). The fact that *The Crucible* was written to address the feeling of being "out of sync" with the time (or of the time *itself* being out of sync)—or that, years later, Miller deemed it necessary to characterize the creation of the work as speaking to such an experience—establishes a relation of referentiality, even when this is done retrospectively and extratextually. What both strengthens and destabilizes the link between Salem and Washington, however, has less to do with the question of whether the play "really" refers to the HUAC hearings and the anti-communist frenzy of the 1950s, and more to do with the fact that productions of the play have tended to "precede and follow revolutions," as Miller himself has noted (xvii). Reference, therefore, does not equate meaning; to dialogue with de Man, despite or in addition to the persistence of a referential moment, the play exhibits a performative or non-cognitive aspect as well. A "meaning" cannot be unearthed from what is perceived as an originary reference or "intentionality" on the part of Miller, but is rather located in the surprise of the event, in which an unanticipated present is shown to be out of joint.

In the introduction to the 2003 publication of the play, Christopher Bigsby states that Miller had been inspired by Marion Starkey's *The Devil in Massachusetts,* which asserts that the events at Salem constituted a "real Greek tragedy . . . with a beginning, a middle and an end" (Bigsby, introduction to *The Crucible,* ix). Like the Inquisition dramas treated here, which typically conclude with an auto-da-fé in which all of the main characters are murdered publicly, Miller's play closes with the impending public execution of John Proctor (while the play insinuates the hanging, the film version depicts his execution as his fellow townspeople look on in horror). Thus not only the tragic in general but a scene of mourning in particular closes each work, establishing an intertextual link with the tradition of the *Trauerspiel* described by Benjamin. The fate of the characters, moreover, is foreshadowed in each work, infusing the entire plot with a limit that frames the story. Over and above a thematic concern, the tragic organizes the *structure* of the plot and, subsequently, of the subjects constituted within it.

I am interested in the way in which this tragic structure ostensibly precludes a relation to the other: here, the other of history, or the other of representation that is annihilated through a conventional reading of allegorical signification. Yet if we are to subscribe to Gabriela Basterra's argument that tragic subjectivity accompanies ethical subjectivity, even while the tragic precludes the ethical, it becomes possible to read in these works a double movement, in which the simultaneous conditions of possibility and impossibility of the opening to the other are present. In her discussion of tragic autonomy versus ethical heteronomy, Basterra asserts that "tragic subjectivity and the ethical demand are based respectively on what would appear to be two different ways of experiencing heteronomy" but clarifies that "these two manifestations of heteronomy might turn out to refer to different perspectives on the same experience" (*Seductions of Fate,* 132). This dynamic, in which the other is only present spectrally, allegorically, will be developed throughout this chapter.

From the beginning, *The Crucible* emphasizes the importance of preserving one's name, linked to a notion of honor that, while originating in premodern society, lingers well into the twentieth century and beyond. The link between reputation and power is announced from the first act of the play, which depicts Reverend Parris as overly preoccupied with his standing in the eyes of the townspeople. Upon witnessing a group of girls from the town dancing in the forest with the West Indian slave Tituba, Parris appears far less concerned about the actual practice of witchcraft than he is worried that his enemies will use the rumors of heresy to destroy him. "They will howl me out of Salem for such corruption in my house," he shouts, "they will topple me with this!" (Miller, *The Crucible*, 13, 15). In the first of many scenes of questioning, Parris grills his niece Abigail, thought to be at the core of the sinful practices, about her name: "Your name in the town—it is entirely white, is it not?", to which Abigail replies, "Why, I am sure it is, sir. There be no blush about my name . . . My name is good in the village! I will not have it said my name is soiled!" (11–12). Reverend Parris then summons Reverend Hale, a known authority on witchcraft, in order to get to the bottom of the mystery of his daughter Betty's speechless state. When Hale questions Tituba and the rest of the girls, he appears interested above all else in gathering names: "When the Devil comes to you does he ever come—with another person? . . . Perhaps another person in the village? Someone you know" (43). Soon enough, Abigail and the now-speaking Betty understand what it is that Hale and the others want and begin to recite names in shrieking voices:

> *Abigail:* . . . I saw Sarah Good with the Devil! I saw Goody Osburn with the Devil! I saw Bridget Bishop with the Devil! . . .
>
> *Betty (staring too)*: I saw George Jacobs with the Devil! I saw Goody Howe with the Devil! . . . I saw Martha Bellows with the Devil! . . .
>
> *Abigail:* I saw Goody Sibber with the Devil! (*It is rising to a great glee.*)
>
> . . .
>
> *Betty:* I saw Alice Barrow with the Devil! . . .
>
> *Abigail:* I saw Goody Hawkins with the Devil! . . .
>
> *Betty:* I saw Goody Bibber with the Devil! . . .
>
> *Abigail:* I saw Goody Booth with the Devil! (Miller, *The Crucible*, 45–46)

The first act ends with names flying as a collective hysteria grips the young girls. While no culprit has yet been identified, identification itself emerges as a performative act through which guilt can be established and, as we shall see, potentially undone.

The second act reveals the foundational transgression of the play: John Proctor's extramarital relationship with the young Abigail. It is this event, of course, that has marred Abigail's name in the town, and that will ultimately lead to Proctor's downfall. John's wife Elizabeth (who knows about the affair) learns that Abigail has named her in the court that has been assembled to accuse those practicing witchcraft in Salem, and believes it to be a sign that her husband has led the young girl to believe they may have a future together: "There be a thousand names: why does she call mine? There be a certain danger in calling such a name—I am no Goody Good that sleeps in ditches, nor Osburn, drunk and half-witted. She'd dare not call out such a farmer's wife but there be monstrous profit in it. She thinks to take my place, John" (Miller, *The Crucible*, 58). The marital fissure that stands at the core of the social rupture that the witch trials create (believing themselves to be suturing it) is described here through the motif of naming. Defending one's name—or conversely, calling out the name of the other—becomes the central act through which subjects and communities are made and unmade.

That naming should serve as a principal link between Salem and Washington (proper names in themselves) deserves reflection. The main objective of the HUAC hearings was, even more than eliciting confessions of communism, securing the names of others. Perhaps the most notorious part of the trials focused upon artists and members of the entertainment industry: the legendary "Hollywood Ten" were fired for suspected communist affiliation, and a longer list of 121 names (including Miller's) were published in *Red Channels*, a right-wing pamphlet. The gravest repercussions of the hearings as well as the more general anti-communist sentiment had less to do with the imprisonment of the accused, and more to do with the reputations that were destroyed as a result: an individual charged with communist sympathizing had a greater chance of losing his or her livelihood than of actually going to jail. Aware of HUAC's interest in compiling a list of communist sympathizers, Miller requested that he not be questioned about colleagues and friends as a condition to participating in the proceedings and confessing his own political involvement, explaining that he was firmly against bringing trouble to others by giving over names.[11] This is vital to the present reading of the play not in a biographical sense but in an intertextual sense: the practice of "naming" that dominated the mid-century anti-communist witch hunt and that Miller rejected in his collaboration with Congress assumes a figurative significance in the theatrical production.

John Proctor's attempt to defend himself while demanding collective justice remains similarly rooted in a desire to purify his name and the names of others (not least that of his wife whom he knows he has wronged). When, near the end of the play, Proctor announces that he has decided to offer a false confession in order to save himself from being hanged, he knows that doing so will preserve his life at the expense of his integrity: "God in Heaven, what is John Proctor, what is John Proctor?" (Miller, *The Crucible*, 127). He refuses Judge Danforth's request that he submit a signed confession to nail to the church door as an example to the town, preferring that his friends and neighbors hear the news from the judges instead because "what others say and what I sign to is not the same" (132). The motif of the signature is crucial here: it marks, beyond the idea of an objective truth that could either be reported or signed, the irreducible singularity of the proper name.

In the most dramatic monologue of the play, Proctor decides to withdraw his confession, explaining in a cry: "Because it is my name! Because I cannot have another in my life! Because I lie and sign myself to lies! Because I am not worth the dust on the feet of them that hang! How may I live without my name? I have given you my soul; leave me my name!" (Miller, *The Crucible*, 133). The fact that while he is ultimately murdered he is able to defend his good name is significant. Indeed, it is only through death that Proctor can preserve his name: not because of the particular details of the circumstances, but because tragic death guarantees the survival of the symbolic order. If this seems counterintuitive, it is. Basterra notes this paradox in her reflection upon the tragic subject's desire for death (which she distinguishes from Freud's death drive): "Having to die in order to become a subject seems an extraordinary thing. . . . What could one gain by desiring to die?" She responds by suggesting that it is only through death that tragic fate is fulfilled: "one becomes a tragic victim by constructing what one imagines that the Other desires (from oneself) as the dictates of fate," so that "we achieve a position in the social system of meaning by assuming guilt" (Basterra, *Seductions of Fate*, 40).

There is therefore a tension in the act of signing—or in the refusal to sign—between fixing meaning and preserving singularity. That John's "goodness" must be protected above all else implies an essentialist understanding of identity as positive content that can or should be safeguarded against corruption. At the same time, there is a subtle resistance to this worldview, conveyed through the motif of the signature. There is an eventual quality to the act of signing one's proper name that prevents total assimilation of Proctor into Judge Danforth, but also of Proctor into Miller, of Salem into Washington. The motif of naming thus marries signifier to signified in an aporetic bind that calls into question

conventional understandings of how historical allegory works. By refusing to sign away his good name, Proctor voices opposition to the all-
consuming power of the court while, on the level of form, resisting an
essentialist reading of historical allegory.

On the level of content, the spectral quality of allegory finds reso-
nance in a story that takes witchcraft as its principal theme. The trials
dramatized by Miller do not abide by the "rational" order of law that
serves as the foundation of the secular courtroom, but instead rely upon
"spectral evidence" to prove guilt. The haunting happens individually
(characters are shown having visions), collectively (the visions are evoked
and affirmed in the courtroom), and narratively (or performatively, as
I will explain below). Elizabeth Proctor describes the strange use of the
spectral in the legal proceedings: "Abigail brings the other girls into the
court, and where she walks the crowd will part like the sea for Israel.
And folks are brought before them, and if they scream and howl and
fall to the floor—the person's clapped in the jail for bewitchin' them"
(Miller, *The Crucible*, 50). Later, the Proctors' maid, Mary Warren, gives
a personal account of having provided spectral evidence herself. In her
description of the experience, she underscores her sense of surprise, as a
memory she never had before suddenly appears to her: "[Sarah Good]
tried to kill me many times . . . I never knew it before. I never knew
anything before. When she come into the court I say to myself, I must
not accuse this woman, for she sleep in ditches, and so very old and
poor. But then—then she sit there, denying and denying, and I feel a
misty coldness climbin' up my back, and the skin on my skull begin to
creep, and I feel a clamp around my neck and I cannot breathe air;
and then—*entranced*—I hear a voice, a screamin' voice, and it were my
voice—and all at once I remember everything she done to me!" (54–55).
Mary conveys her testimony as if it came from another ("I hear a voice
. . . and it were my voice"), and her memory as something that unexpectedly possesses her ("I never knew it before"). Memory, commonly
thought to point to a past moment, appears here to arrive as if from
the future. Derrida affirms this unlikely conjugation of past and future
in his description of the specter as returning from "the past as absolute
future," underscoring the fact that what we perceive as historical arrives
in the present moment, taking us by surprise.[12] In Mary's case, an experience from the past (Sarah Good mumbling to herself after Mary has
turned her away without food) returns to the present bearing a completely new meaning (a curse that causes her illness); the free-floating
signifier of the encounter with Sarah Good allows the past to be read as

future. Of course, the validity of Mary's claim is represented as shaky at best (John's authoritative voice protests, "But the proof, the proof!") but it seems quite clear that Mary believes *herself* to be haunted. The inclusion of spectral evidence in Miller's work simultaneously exposes the irrationality of the witch hunt, discrediting the testimony as false or imagined, while underscoring the very real fear that grips the young girls (and, by extension, the entire town).

Beyond the scenes that thematize spectrality on a constative level, haunting infuses the entire work performatively through the use of allegory. Miller's employment of historical allegory does not merely draw a parallel between the collective hysteria and persecution of innocents in the seventeenth and twentieth centuries, it exposes the anachronistic quality of the present, that which does not quite fit and therefore that which is untimely about the present. The fact that McCarthyism can be linked figuratively to the witch trials reveals a *ritual religiosity* and *affective panic* at work in the twentieth century, a time that would ostensibly be characterized by secularism and rationality rather than affect or faith. It is then—unpredictably—repeated in each successive production, which articulates a previously unanticipated instantiation of untimeliness. We cannot therefore fix a meaning in the "original" version of *The Crucible*; its meaning only comes about unexpectedly, from the future: in the foreshadowing (to return to the example that opens this chapter) of an anachronistic division of the world into good and evil, the logic that continues to guide hegemonic power since 9/11. Just as the act of naming—which ties Salem to Washington even as it maintains the singularity of each—bears an aporetic quality in its simultaneous fixing of meaning and defense of singularity, the "original" script's allegorical meaning turns out to be incomplete, necessarily fragmented or partial because "the allegorical must constantly unfold in new and surprising ways" (Benjamin, *Origin of German Tragic Drama*, 183). Allegory allows for multiple potential meanings-to-come: and who knows what line will resonate in some as-yet-undetermined future moment?

Specters of Tlatelolco

In several of the late-twentieth-century Inquisition narratives discussed in the present book, it is possible to detect a turn to historical allegory reminiscent of that which we have witnessed in Miller. The situating of action within the historical moment of the Inquisition in Ripstein's *El Santo Oficio*, Berman's *En el nombre de Dios,* and Santareno's O

Judeu, in particular, exemplifies the dynamic that Miller employs in its reliance upon historical difference to assume a critical position vis-à-vis the present. Yet I want to downplay the idea of intentionality inherent in this move, whether understood as aesthetic or political. Rather than focusing upon authorial intent, I would instead underscore the unexpected, surprising elements of these dramatic works that exceed the overdetermined relationship of equivalence between past and present.

The plot of Ripstein's *El Santo Oficio,* as I argue in the previous chapter, is framed by death: the film opens at Rodrigo de Carvajal's funeral (the Jewishness of which will seal the fate of the marrano family) and concludes with the public burning of Luis de Carvajal along with his entire family and immediate community, whom he has denounced under torture. The tone of mourning that permeates the work beginning with the funeral scene—"Francisca permanece inmóvil," "Mariana gime en el hombro de Justa Méndez," "todos . . . visten cuidadosa pero modestamente" ("Francisca remains frozen, Mariana whimpers into the shoulder of Justa Méndez, everyone is dressed carefully and modestly") (Ripstein and Pacheco, *El Santo Oficio,* 13)—is fundamental to its allegorical quality. Yet I want to suggest that Rodrigo's funeral alludes to a fatality or fatalism that goes beyond the individual death of the father. The question then becomes: *what* or *whom* is mourned here? What is the loss around which Ripstein's film is structured? Is it possible to identify, in addition to the myriad deaths of crypto-Jews at the hands of the Inquisition, a secondary or *supplementary* death that haunts the film? Put another way: what is being mourned in late-twentieth-century Mexico that cannot be named directly and must be articulated through the lens of the Inquisition? While in the next chapter I will critique the logic of "truth-telling" under torture according to which the truth is ultimately *sayable,* I want to argue here in favor of an alternative discourse of the unsaid or the *unsayable,* intimately tied to the allegorical form the work takes.

If we are to pursue the idea that there is a dynamic at play in allegory that moves beyond the model of the masquerade or the logic of *alêtheia,* that it is possible to read allegory as that which exceeds or subverts the relationship between signifier and signified, mask and face, it is necessary to mine the margins of the work. The central conflict of the film is situated between New Christians and Old Christians or, more precisely, between the Carvajals and their community, on the one hand, and the Inquisition authorities, on the other. The majority of the action takes place either within the crypto-Jewish community or in the ecclesiastical institutions and Inquisitorial prison, and the characters are principally *peninsulares* (Spaniards and Portuguese) and *criollos* (ethnic Europeans born in the Americas). Yet the broader sociopolitical context of colonial Mexico does not escape the film: Ripstein situates the specific story of the Carvajals within the more general (and more complex) dynamic of race and ethnicity, economics and power in sixteenth-century Mexico. Populating the periphery of the action are the indigenous peoples that served as the main target of colonial violence (and who can also be read as conversos, having been forcibly converted as part of the process of colonization).

After the entire Carvajal family is arrested by Inquisition authorities, Luis's brother Baltasar—the only relative to escape—goes into hiding with Gregorio López, a reclusive mystic and an ally of crypto-Jews and other accused heretics. The scene opens outside López's adobe hut as a group of peasants dash through the forest; the screenplay indicates that "una veintena de mujeres, hombres y niños—todos indígenas o mestizos, vestidos con indecible pobreza—atraviesan el bosque. Huyen como si alguien o algo los persiguiera" ("Some twenty women, men and children— all indigenous or mestizos, dressed with unspeakable poverty—traverse the forest. They flee as if someone or something were following them") (Ripstein and Pacheco, *El Santo Oficio*, 34). The person or thing thought to be pursuing the peasants is narrated using the subjunctive and is never named outright, yet its presence is felt (perhaps even more strongly) due to the ambiguity with which it is described. This unnamed enemy, together with the "indecible pobreza" displayed by the indigeous and mestizo peasants, alludes to an "other side" of the narrated or narratable story. The unmentionable nature of their condition is specified in writing by the screenplay (and is therefore graphically "readable" in the published version of the screenplay), but remains unspoken in the film itself, which relies on the visual to portray the poverty and peril in which the peasants live. This silence is repeated within López's hut: when Baltasar asks Gregorio what will happen to his family, the hermit is mute: "En vez de contestar Gregorio López se sirve un vaso de agua" ("Instead of answering Gregorio López pours himself a glass of water") (35).

The motif of silence is revisited in a later scene that follows the torture and rape of Luis's sister Mariana in prison and subsequent release of the Carvajal family. Mariana is depicted as having lost her reason, screaming that she would rather die than return to prison and to the abuse she suffered at the hands of the prison guards. She takes an image of San Cristóbal and hurls it over the balcony into the street while the screenplay specifies that "dos indígenas a quienes no parece importar lo que ocurre se encuentran recargados en la pared de enfrente. Luis sale a la calle y se inclina a recoger el santo que se ha desbaratado con la caída. Vuelve a entrar en la casa mientras se escuchan los gritos de Mariana" ("two indigenous men who don't seem concerned with what is happening recline against the wall outside. Luis goes out to the street to recover the saint that has broken with the fall. He reenters the house as Mariana's cries are heard from within") (Ripstein and Pacheco, *El Santo Oficio*, 77–78). The presence of the sedentary men outside the house portrays the "Indian" as at once peripheral to the main plot and symbolically essential to the interrelated projects of Inquisition and colonialism. The Catholic icon is shattered and then recovered by Luis, while the silent image of the two indigenous men remains unscathed. The juxtaposition of the ruined image of the saint (amidst decidedly loud cries of agony) with the silent, passive Indians signals a fracturing of Catholicism while maintaining the figure of the "Indian" intact.

These two scenes, together with the scene I discuss in the previous chapter, in which *el Mozo* unsuccessfully attempts to convert a group of indigenous men and boys he sees on their way to church, posit *lo indígena* as an alternate history that supplements the main history of Jewish conversion and persecution.[13] In each example, the subplot seems to shadow or accompany the central plot: the group of "indigenous and mestizos" hurry through the forest just as Baltasar flees to Gregorio López's remote hut; two "indigenous men" sit silently as the crypto-Jewish Mariana screams in fear; Luis tries to convert a group of "indigenous men and women" immediately following his own awakening. The device of shadowing establishes a crucial link between Inquisition and conquest: the expulsions, conversions, and Inquisitions that found early modern Spanish and Portuguese nationhood on one side of the Atlantic are portrayed as necessarily tied to the conversion, enslavement, and massacre of indigenous peoples in the newly settled colonies on the other. The last example insinuates a relationship between religious persecution and the broader ethnic and economic violence of the conquest. Here, the precise wording of *el Mozo* as he attempts to convert the group is significant: "Les quitaron todo y les inculcan mentiras para hacerlos pensar como ellos. Quieren abusar y humillarlos a su antojo. La tierra es de ustedes. Así lo dispuso Adonay, único Dios verdadero" ("They stole everything from you and they teach you lies to make you think like them. They want to abuse and humiliate you at their whim. The land is yours. That is the way Adonay, the only true God, made it") (Ripstein and Pacheco, *El Santo Oficio*, 84). In this passage, religious rhetoric is woven together with a Marxist discourse of sorts: the land belongs to those who work it because God has created the world in that way. This hybrid rhetoric links past and present injustices: the violent conquest, which leads to a corrupt present, reappears within the present to expose that "the time is out of joint." The postcolonial quality of PRI-dominated twentieth-century Mexico (implied only indirectly here) means that the Mexican Revolution's promise of land to "the people" (meant to correct the crimes of colonialism) has remained unfulfilled. Stolen land, here, metonymically signals a broader loss or void at the heart of the conquest that returns to haunt the present through allegory.

Land—or geography understood more broadly—becomes increasingly significant as the plot develops. After the Carvajal family has been freed, the setting shifts from prison to a house in the Tlatelolco section of Mexico City, where Francisca and Mariana now live and where their community gathers to observe Jewish rituals clandestinely. The choice of location is highly significant: *El Santo Oficio*, which premiered in 1974, was penned in the wake of the 1968 massacre of hundreds of students at the Plaza de las Tres Culturas in Tlatelolco.[14] The plaza, surrounded on three sides by an Aztec archaeological excavation site, houses the ruins of an earlier, foundational violence: the subjugation of indigenous peasants in colonial Mexico. The significance of Tlatelolco is culturally specific, so that an allegorical reading of the scene depends upon a decidedly local knowledge of history. To the outsider, Tlatelolco remains an anonymous site while to an "informed" viewer the scene conjures up a series of traumatic events that reverberate into the present. Although the published screenplay names the setting directly ("CASA EN TLATELOLCO"), the film version requires an even more intimate knowledge of the place. In this sense, the visual works in an oblique manner, situating the action in Tlatelolco without directly naming it, thereby subverting the representational structure inherent to a conventional understanding of allegory and adding a haunting quality to the allegorical. This is not to say that the visual always heralds a suspension of identity: indeed, the very notion of "hauntology" plays on the visually present but aurally indistinguishable difference between *hantologie* and *ontologie,* between haunting and being. That the ruins of pre-Columbian Mexico encase the modern-day Plaza de las Tres Culturas creates an uncomfortable juxtaposition of past and present, and reminds us of the necessary bond between allegory, ruins, and haunting.

At the same time, the fact that the indigenous "characters" (they are so one-dimensional they can hardly be called characters) are represented as mute and ignorant ("El joven ríe sin entender las palabras de Luis") introduces a significant constraint to the dynamic of haunting. If the specter exposes the untimely quality of the present, the essentialist rendering of the subaltern imposes a limit to the deconstructive potential of hauntology. While the indigenous subplot offers an additional dimension to the main plot, it ultimately proves instrumental: the "Indian" acts as a rhetorical figure that supplements the Inquisition story while remaining rooted in an identitarian logic that fails to subvert any meaning one could extract from the film.

In a sense we can understand this aporetic dynamic as connected to the contradiction at the heart of the marrano subject. As I argue in the previous chapter, there is a tension that permeates the rhetoric of *marranismo* between purity and resistance, identity and anti-identity (rather than identity and difference), readability and unreadability, between the successful and unsuccessful conversion of the other. These contradictory logics or registers—ideological, religious, or philosophical—are ultimately inseparable, so that the discourse of purity makes subversion impossible and the discourse of subversion deconstructs purity. Likewise, these Inquisition stories oscillate between relying on a decidedly referential understanding of language, on the one hand, and signaling an exteriority (or an exteriority within) that cannot be fully assimilated by the text.

Allegory, Parody, Performance

In contrast to Ripstein's problematic thematization of *lo indígena,* Sabina Berman adds a degree of texture to the indigenous characters that populate *En el nombre de Dios* and, in doing so, expands the potential of the allegorical work as spectral—specifically, the ethico-political inflection of the demand posed by the specter (Derrida, *Specters of Marx,* 22). Like Ripstein, Berman situates the Carvajal story within the broader ethnic, social, and political milieu of colonial Mexico, establishing a similar link between past and present. But Berman's "Indians" are neither mute nor ignorant: through the use of parody, Berman portrays Juan and Pedro as three-dimensional characters, and the colonial authority that fears them as ignorant. The "voyage within" Mexico—Luisito's journey to Jojutla and his enemies' reaction to the town during Semana Santa—serves as a second instance in which the problem of colonial subjectivity is unpacked through the allegorical figures of the crypto-Jew and "crypto-Indian."

Don Luis's servants Juan and Pedro appear for the first time in act 1, scene 5, in which Don Luis meets with Padre Jeremías at the Palace of the Holy Inquisition. As Don Luis and his servants kneel before the priest, Padre Jeremías's absurdity is made apparent through his encounter with the "savages."

Padre Jeremías: Chichi-macas.

Don Luis va a sentarse junto al Padre.

Don Luis: Chichi-mecas, padre Jeremías. Le cuidarán con esmero. Le harán música cuando convenga y cuando convenga le cargarán los baúles, a usted que viene y va por las colonias del Imperio.

Padre Jeremías (en secreto a don Luis): Pero ¿no le oí decir el otro día que son bárbaros, comedores de gente?

Don Luis: No. Sus padres lo fueron. Juan y Pedro se criaron ya en mi hacienda en Tampico. Son dóciles, musicales y muy cristianos.

Juan y Pedro enseñan los dientes.

Padre Jeremías (alarmado): ¿Qué les pasa?

Don Luis: Están sonriendo.

Padre Jeremías: Ah, vaya. ¿Y esa fruta viene con ellos? ¿Es lo que comen?

Don Luis: Comen de todo. Los plátanos son otro regalo, su Senoría.

Juan (corta un plátano y empieza a pelarlo): ¿Quiere, su Santísimo?

Padre Jeremías (jubiloso y nervioso a la vez): ¡Habla castellano! No. Cómela tú, criatura. (*Para el padre, Juan y Pedro son exóticos animalitos: ¿peligrosos?, ¿qué tan humanos?*) (Berman, *En el nombre de Dios,* 334–35)

Padre Jeremías: Chichi-macas.

Don Luis takes a seat next to the priest.

Don Luis: Chichi-mecas, Father Jeremías. They will take excellent care of you. They will play music for you when you so desire and when you need it they will carry your trunks, for you who comes and goes through the colonies of the Empire.

Padre Jeremías (whispering to Don Luis): But didn't I hear the other day that they're barbarians, cannibals?

Don Luis: No. Their parents were. Juan and Pedro were raised on my estate in Tampico. They are docile, musical and very Christian.

Juan and Pedro bare their teeth.

Padre Jeremías (alarmed): What's wrong with them?

Don Luis: They're smiling.

Padre Jeremías: Oh—well. And that fruit comes with them? That's what they eat?

Don Luis: They eat everything. The bananas are another gift, your Highness.

Juan (cuts a banana and begins to peel it): Would you like some, your Holiness?

Padre Jeremías (at once jubilant and nervous): He speaks Spanish! No. You eat it, creature. (*To the priest, Juan and Pedro are exotic animals: dangerous?, how human?*)[15]

In this scene, it is Padre Jeremías who appears ignorant despite his position of dominance: he calls Juan and Pedro "chichi-macas" rather than *chichimecas* (itself a pejorative term used by the Nahua peoples to refer to a range of indigenous groups from northern Mexico), does not know what a banana is, misreads their smiles, and appears simultaneously comforted and spooked by their ability to speak Spanish. While the servants are portrayed humorously (they bare their teeth rather than smiling), their "almost the same, but not quite" mimetic quality (reminiscent of the colonial mimicry described by Homi Bhabha) does not reveal them to be ridiculous but rather exposes the gap intrinsic to the unequal relation between colonizer and colonized (Berman, *En el nombre de Dios*, 126). Likewise, their fluency in Spanish inspires ambivalence in the priest because while their conversion has been "successful" (they no longer practice cannibalism, they speak a European tongue), the *similarity* between colonizer and colonized is (at least to those in power) even more threatening than its absence. The stage directions at the end of the passage convey the priest's fear of the exotic beings that face him: the question marks ("*¿peligrosos?, ¿qué tan humanos?*") indicate an instability inherent to colonial hegemony.

Berman also goes further than Ripstein in establishing a relationship between Inquisition and colonialism. If in Ripstein's film the conquest of New Spain serves as a backdrop to the more central plot of Inquisitorial violence, in Berman's play one mode of violence does not eclipse the other, but rather each relation of power serves to corroborate and sustain the other. The above-mentioned scene situates Don Luis within the broader colonial power dynamic: he is a governor, a landowner, a slaveowner. Yet while he belongs to the economic and political elite, it is his very power that turns him into a victim of the Inquisition. Crypto-Jewish settler and enslaved *chichimeca* are not equal, but both ultimately play into the hands of the Old Christian peninsular elite.

The compatibility of Jewish and indigenous conversion becomes more evident in the scene that I discuss in the previous chapter, in which Luisito goes to Jojutla to work with his missionary brother. As I have already argued, the entire Jojutla "scene" (the village itself resembles a theater) offers a reading of marrano subjectivity in which no identitary essence can be said to reside beneath the disguise. Identity in general, and crypto-Jewish identity in particular, is represented as a performance in the most expansive sense of the word, perhaps best articulated through Samuel Weber's notion of theatricality.[16] Indigenous identity also bears a performative quality within the colonial context: in Jojutla, religious syncretism and cultural hybridity take the form of masquerade. Indians appear costumed, churches are painted brightly, and Catholic rites are translated and transformed ("Nuevo Mundo, rituales nuevos," remarks the Carvajal family lawyer [Berman, *En el nombre de Dios,* 369]). The decidedly allegorical quality of Semana Santa opens up a broad array of possible meanings, of which the constitutively heretical nature of Christianity represents but one.

The Carvajal family attorney and Felipe Nuñez (Don Luis's subordinate, who plots to replace *el Mozo* as heir to the Carvajal fortune) independently travel to Jojutla in order to gather evidence of Luisito's heresy. Upon arrival, they are immediately confronted with a town-wide celebration of Holy Week, in which Indians walk the streets dressed as Romans and the role of Jesus is played by none other than *el Mozo* himself. As Luisito emerges bearing a cross, the Dominican friars shout blasphemous epithets while Felipe and the attorney observe in bewilderment:

> *Dominico* 1: Bájate de la cruz, si eres el hijo de Dios.
>
> *Dominico* 2: Venías a salvarnos, y a ti mismo no te puedes salvar.
>
> *Abogado*: Estas blasfemias son bíblicas. Aparecen en los Evangelios.
>
> *Dominico* 3: ¡Sácate los clavos, Mesías!
>
> *Dominico* 4: Rey de los judíos.
>
> *Felipe Nuñez*: ¿Bíblicas?
>
> *Abogado*: Muy bíblicas. (Berman, *En el nombre de Dios,* 371)

> *Dominican* 1: Get down off the cross, if you're the son of God.
>
> *Dominican* 2: You came to save us, and you can't even save yourself.
>
> *Lawyer:* These blasphemies are biblical. They appear in the Evangelios.
>
> *Dominican* 3: Take out those nails, Messiah!
>
> *Dominican* 4: King of the Jews.
>
> *Felipe Nuñez:* Biblical?
>
> *Lawyer:* Very biblical.

The claim that the blasphemies uttered by the friars originate in the Christian Bible itself—the positing of Christianity as always already heretical—suggests that the masquerade is not a sufficient model for identity, that every projection of identity (religious, ethnic, or otherwise) contains an inevitable breach at its core. It is through allegory—a performative allegory, one that is realized not only in time but "live"—that the essence of Christianity (and thus the authority of the Old Christian) is deconstructed. That this performative allegory relies on the figurative conjugation of crypto-Jew and *chichimeca* implies a complicity that extends to the present day, into PRI-dominated Mexico, immediately preceding the neo-Zapatista uprising in Chiapas in 1994.

Interestingly, the entire indigenous component is virtually absent from the earlier 1983 version of the play *Herejía* (with the exception of a brief scene in which Jesús Baltazar whips a *chichimeca* slave), so that the allegorical quality of the work comes about only through the process of revision. Allegory can therefore be understood to have a profoundly contemporary significance: in rewriting the play to include a more politically relevant dimension, it becomes necessary to resort to the allegorical. Revision, which here instantiates a sort of making-present or re-presentation, relies upon historical allegory precisely in order to enable the play to move *beyond* the past. It therefore ceases to be a play "about" the Inquisition at the very moment that it gestures toward something other than itself.

Allegory, Anachronism, Apostrophe

Both Ripstein's film and Berman's play depart from the allegorical structure employed by Miller in their incorporation of a secondary or supplementary plot into the main story. If in Miller the McCarthy hearings remain external to the theatrical work (the present is addressed abstractly, through empty signifiers), Ripstein and Berman integrate a subaltern narrative into the plot, albeit peripherally. What remains absent from all three examples is the present—an untimely, unanticipated present that is called into question by the conflicts dramatized by the performative works. Because the "present"—an empty signifier in itself—is in constant motion and as such impossible to fix, each production or screening encounters a new and therefore wholly unpredictable social, political, and aesthetic moment. Bernardo Santareno's 1966 play *O Judeu* serves as the sole example within this corpus of Inquisition allegories of a work that explicitly addresses the present but, in doing so, risks the foreclosure of possible meanings. Through the figure of the time-traveling narrator and the prophetic dreams of António José's mother, Lourença, *O Judeu* addresses the totalitarianism and genocide of twentieth-century Europe through the use of apostrophe and the visual.

A dramatic narrative penned during the repressive Salazar dictatorship in mid-twentieth-century Portugal but not performed until after Santareno's death in 1980, *O Judeu* belongs to a broader tradition of Inquisition dramas written or performed under totalitarian regimes and, as such, serves as a bold voice of resistance to fascism. By establishing a link between past and present "unenlightened" political cultures through allegory, Santareno—whose 1959 *O crime da Aldeia Velha* also dramatizes a frenzied witch hunt—appropriates the singularity of the Inquisition in a universalizing gesture that equates distinct historical moments. This move, while not entirely dissimilar from Miller's denunciation of McCarthyism through the lens of the Salem Witch Trials or Ripstein's and Berman's critique of PRI-dominated Mexico, goes a step further in speaking directly to a "contemporary" viewer and in explicitly naming then contemporary Portugal and the Holocaust as part of its condemnation of twentieth-century fascism. Through an analysis of the narrative function of the Cavaleiro de Oliveira and the disturbing prophesies of Lourença, I want to explore the relationship between apostrophe, visuality, and haunting, asking if the work remains limited to the realm of the "sayable" or whether it is possible for narrative address and visual projections to perturb the public by pointing to another side of the spoken story.

I have already discussed in the previous chapter the way in which Santareno displaces the *marranismo* of António José onto the (also converted) narrator Cavaleiro de Oliveira. Oliveira's Protestantism is doubly significant in its metonymic signaling of the "enlightened" quality of northern Europe, which stands in contrast to the "backwards" religious and cultural milieu of eighteenth-century Portugal. Santareno portrays Portugal as lagging behind the then-modernizing European continent and Britain, which is why, as I have noted, the narrator speaks from his position of exile in a more modern London. As a writer, Oliveira serves as a voice of authority on cultural and political matters alike. While the narrator refers to a period of potential cultural wealth in Portugal (he describes the "século das luzes" ushered in by the gold and diamonds acquired from Brazil), he does so only ironically; the riches garnered from the Portuguese colonies, rather than producing a culture of cosmopolitan modernity, instead relegates Portugal to a premodern, uncivilized state consumed with battles for power amongst religious, political, and economic elites. Speaking from London, he condemns the darkness in which Portugal lives and which, if allowed to continue, will lead to its downfall:

> "É preciso resgatar os portugueses do jugo nefando do Santo Ofício. Vai nisso a salvação do reino, pois que ciências e artes a par e passo do progresso, civilidade e civilização, um comércio próspero, uma autoridade cônscia das suas fun-ções, uma religião purgada de idolatria, enfim, portugueses ilustrados e conscientes, não poderá haver enquanto perdure a monstruosa jurisdição!" (Santareno, O Judeu, 46)

> "It is necessary to rescue the Portuguese from the evil yoke of the Holy Office. In this lies the salvation of the kingdom, indeed, sciences and arts on par with progress, civility and civilization, a prosperous commerce, an authority cognizant of its responsibilities, a religion purged of idolatry, in sum, an enlightened and aware Portuguese people, cannot exist as long as this monstruous jurisdiction endures!"

It is the Holy Office, according to Oliveira, that stands as the barrier to progress and enlightenment in the Iberian nation, though in what follows this pronouncement will be called into question as the singularity of the Inquisition is supplanted by successive incarnations of terror.

At the same time that Santareno imbues the narrator with the authority to relate and, subsequently, to judge the state of affairs in eighteenth-century Portugal, he relativizes this authority by exposing Oliveira's character flaws and by introducing a limit to narrative discourse through the visual. A confessed narcissist, the narrator admits that despite his penchant for storytelling, he has remained a "minor" writer because he can't stop talking about himself: "Eu escrevo porque . . . porque gosto de falar de mim, é certo" ("I write because . . . because I enjoy talking about myself, it's true") (Santareno, *O Judeu*, 47). In addition to the narrator's status as a "minor" writer, Santareno portrays Oliveira's verbal acumen as insufficient to convey the whole story, so that as he is endlessly dissertating on the evils of the Inquisition, it is António José who illustrates the narrator's point by displaying his wounded wrists—the result of torture at the hands of the Inquisition—to the audience. Here, the visual displaces the verbal as dominant discourse: showing trumps telling.

Perhaps for this reason, the function of the narrator goes beyond the contours of character and the discourse pronounced by him to include the performative dimension of his role. The performative, in Santareno, proves as vital to the meaning of the play as the cognitive, so that what Oliveira says must be read alongside the way in which he says it, and to whom. The temporal distance the narrator traverses in his excessively long monologues is realized through the rhetorical tool of apostrophe, from the Greek *apostrophé* or "turning away." In several crucial moments of the dramatic narrative, Oliveira stops and turns to speak directly to the audience, addressing an imagined or idealized "enlightened" Portuguese public. Here, linear temporality is suspended in favor of a simultaneity of past and present; while the narrator lives in the eighteenth century, he first imagines and then invokes a twentieth-century interlocutor: "Estou a pensar . . . sim, quanto daria eu para saber como estarão estas cousas, as celestes e as terrenas, lá para diante, no tempo vindouro . . . daqui a duzentos anos?! . . . Respondei-me vós, portugueses do século xx: vós que, para mim, sois sombras fugidias da esperança e do temor! Como será? . . ." ("I wonder . . . yes, what I wouldn't give to know how these matters, both celestial and earthly, will turn out in the future . . . two hundred years from now?! . . . Answer me, you, Portuguese people of the twentieth century: you who, for me, are fugitive shadows of hope and of fear! How will it be? . . .") (Santareno, *O Judeu*, 55). The pivotal moment in this address comes about through the pronunciation of the words "Respondei-me vós," an interpellation that places an ethical demand on the spectator. Much later in the play, the narrator once again turns his thoughts and discourse to the twentieth century: "E vós outros, portugueses ilustrados e livres, que todos o sereis nesse formoso século XX, se acaso os lerdes . . . haveis de nos pensar e lamentar" ("And you, enlightened and free Portuguese, as you

all will be in that beautiful twentieth century, if by chance you read this
. . . you must think of us and pity us") (217–18). Here the demand is less
radical, the appeal to the "vós" of the present is more of a request than a
command, but the irony inherent in the words "ilustrados" and "livres"
suggests that there is more to the idealization of the twentieth-century
public than meets the eye.

In two further moments of juxtaposition between the eighteenth and
twentieth centuries, the narrator imagines the public to be a necessarily
critical reader of history: "Penso . . . imagino qual o julgamento que das
gentes altas do meu tempo hão de fazer os portugueses vindouros que
isto lerem, ou ouvirem contar? Aqueles felizes mortais que terão a dita
imerecida de viver no Portugal do século xx?" ("I think . . . I wonder
how will the future Portuguese that read this, or hear about this, judge
the elite of my time? Those happy mortals who have the undeserved
luck to live in the Portugal of the twentieth century?") (Santareno, O
Judeu, 95), and later, "como tudo isto há-de parecer estranho, absurdo
mesmo, aos portugueses que viverão daqui a cem, duzentos anos . . .
nesse progressivo, inteligente e livre século xx!" ("how strange, how
truly absurd, this all must seem to the Portuguese who will live one,
two hundred years from now . . . in that progressive, intelligent and free
twentieth century!") (188). There is a sort of reverse anachronism at
work here; rather than illustrating a productive divide between past and
present, the narrative apostrophe instead exposes the untimeliness of
the present, the anti-progressive, anti-liberal impulses of an ostensibly
enlightened epoch.

The performance of difference, the false dichotomy between past
and present staged by the narrator, is further bridged by a gesture of
sameness through the visual. As the third act opens, the stage directions
specify that the adoring, laughing public that attends Antônio José's
raucous puppet operas encounter a menacing, foreboding tone: "Hão-
de sentir-se pesar como uma sombra pressaga escondida no riso, uma
ameaça sonâmbula, incorpórea, e ambígua" ("They will feel the weight
of an ominous shadow hidden in the laughter, a sonambulent threat,
incorporeal, ambiguous") (Santareno, O Judeu, 171). A haunting tone
characterizes the scene, which shows Antônio José's mother Lourença
screaming in her sleep, engulfed in a nightmare. A visual projection
then appears above the stage showing clips from films documenting
the Nazi concentration camps. The stage directions specify that brutal
scenes of Jews massacred in gas chambers be shown to the audience:
"Massas imensas de vítimas, esfarrapadas ou nuas, movendo-se como

num pesadelo, sem elementos precisos no vestuário, ou outros, capazes de as temporalizar numa época determinada. Pormenores de horror: *O medo angélico das crianças, o rosto da morte nos seres jovens e belos, o misticismo messiânico dos velhos*" ("Immense masses of victims, tattered or naked, moving around like in a nightmare, without clothing or other traits that could locate them in a determined time period. Details of *horror:* the angelic fear of the children, the face of death in the young and beautiful figures, the messianic mysticism of the elders") (172). At the same time that these images are displayed, a voice from offstage lists the names of concentration camps. In this disturbing scene, the progress and reason of the twentieth century are decisively aborted by the images and disembodied narration.

The narrative address, together with the projection of images, assumes the form of both accusation and demand: the spectator is guilty insofar as she is a potential witness to the crimes of the Inquisition and the Holocaust (as well as other, future, unnamed crimes). Santareno establishes the foundation for such a relationship from the outset: the stage directions for the opening scene—an auto-da-fé—position the viewing public as spectators to the public murder of Inquisitorial victims. In the Holocaust scene, the spectator's role as potential witness is further cemented as she is haunted by the images and voice. Here, the coexistence of visual embodiment and verbal disembodiment creates the simultaneous conditions of possibility and impossibility of the haunting of the present. On the one hand, the spectral quality of the voice requires a visible body in order to properly name the proper name of Nazi violence. Yet the "angelic," "beautiful," "messianic," and mystical characteristics of the victims add a sublime quality to the suffering. The direct naming of the present by Santareno, too, limits the deconstructive potential of the allegorical, so that in haunting the present, allegory improperly names the impropriety of the present. It is the explicit references to the (future) present that date Santareno's work, while it is in the historical that the capacity to surprise can be found.

In all four works discussed in this chapter, an uncomfortable rapport between past and present comes about through the use of allegory. Such rhetorical anachronism—realized here through the performative media of theater and film—employs the spectral in order to disrupt the present, or to bring attention to the disruption that is always already a part of the present. Yet there is a tension inherent to the production of historical allegory, which simultaneously gestures toward the other while insisting upon the same. In Miller, the act of naming embodies this double bind between complicity with power, assimilation into the same, on the one hand, and the event of singularity, which would resist such assimilation. Ripstein's film, too, demonstrates a profoundly ambivalent attitude toward sense-making through its use of silences: while in some scenes the silences are embodied by a readable, thematized subaltern, other moments allude to that which remains unspeakable (Derrida's unnameable—or "almost unnameable"—specter). Berman's return to the story of the Carvajals to address contemporary ethnic inequality in Mexico draws upon the deconstructive potential of historical allegory by highlighting the performative aspect of identity and parodying the position of the colonizer. Santareno, unlike Ripstein and Berman, explicitly incorporates the present by interpellating the contemporary viewer, so that historical allegory at once limits and broadens possibilities of interpretation. In all four works, there remains an unresolvable tension between a more conventional reading of allegory and de Man's assertion that allegories "are always allegories of the impossibility of reading" (*Allegories of Reading*, 205). The aporetic nature of sense-making in these works suggests that historical allegory operates on ethically and politically shaky ground. *The Crucible, El Santo Oficio, En el nombre de Dios,* and *O Judeu* all draw upon the claustrophobic identitary narrowness that characterizes Inquisitional logic while at the same time gesturing toward the unreadable, ultimately signaling—albeit obliquely—a tentative ethics and aesthetics of the impossible.

CHAPTER 3

Interrogative Signs

The subject is the void of the impossibility of answering the
question of the Other.
—Slavoj Žižek

The previous two chapters have detailed the way in which constructions
of *marranismo* revolve around that which is fundamentally unknowable in the other, and how Inquisition allegories guard within them the
spectral ruins of a traumatic history. Both the New Christian and allegory, I suggest, retain an untranslatable kernel of otherness: the Jewish
other, the other of history, the other within the same. Yet conventional
understandings of *marranismo* and allegory continue to rely upon the
logic of masquerade, in which both marrano and allegory disguise the
truth by "praying" or "saying" otherwise. The present chapter builds
upon the parallel phenomena of *marranismo* and allegory by taking
a sustained look at aesthetic scenes of Inquisitorial interrogation, the
act by which the violent conversion of Jews is radicalized. I claim that
interrogation exhibits a certain compatibility, or complicity, with *marranismo* and allegory because, returning to Jean-Paul Sartre, the desired
goal of torture is to force from the body of the other "the secret of *everything*" (preface to *The Question*, 23). The marrano, allegory, and interrogation all guard within them an idea of the secret, the unreadable,
or the unsayable, which *inspires* these religious, cultural, and political
practices while at the same time guaranteeing their impossibility.

If the New Christian mask does not in fact conceal an "authentically"
Jewish face, just as allegory does not hide the "true" story (which, under
other conditions, could be related without fear), if *marranismo,* like the
allegorical, hides nothing more than the fact that there is "nothing" to
hide, how are we to understand the act of interrogation, the motive of
which is to uncover the secret of everything? If there is no secret, or if the

87

secret that lies at the heart of the other (of the subject, of narrative, etc.) exceeds representation, what purpose does torture serve, what subject is interrogated and what truth confessed? What is desired in interrogation—by interrogator and interrogated alike—and what (desiring) subject is constituted in the act of confession, in turning toward the Law? This chapter takes a final look at the Inquisition narratives discussed in the previous chapters in order to understand the way in which the aesthetic representation of interrogation oscillates between an avowal and disavowal of the spectral quality of *marranismo*, understood here to be the secret of the other (or of the other within the same). I explore the way in which many of these narratives reproduce Inquisitional logic in scenes depicting torture and confession—despite taking a moral or ideological stance that would indicate the contrary—and ask whether it is possible to signal an excess, or internal limit, to this logic through the language of the aesthetic.

The inherently discursive nature of the act of questioning, as well as the subject that is constituted through this act, serves as the point of departure for my discussion. In the first section of this chapter, I trace the presence of confessional discourse through the realms of the legal, the literary, and the religious, following the recent work of Peter Brooks (*Troubling Confessions*). Considering Brooks's argument that within the Western tradition, confession becomes the means by which the "individual authenticates his inner truth," together with Paul de Man's deconstructive reading of Rousseau's *Confessions* as desire for exposure, I aim to highlight the decidedly literary quality of the confession, as well as of the narrative subject that is constituted through the performative act of confession. If the confession necessarily bears a literary or fictional quality, what does the fictional representation of confession do to our understanding of this practice? I analyze several confessional scenes in Gonçalves de Magalhães's *O poeta e a inquisição* in order to investigate the way in which literary discourse can simultaneously profess innocence while performing guilt.

In the second section of this chapter, I ask whether confession necessarily responds to the positing of a question—whether explicit or implicit—by exploring literary scenes of Inquisitorial questioning. Can we understand the dynamic of interrogation as a form of ideological interpellation in an Althusserian sense? In what way is modern subjectivity premised upon the "turning" of the individual toward the Law, as in Louis Althusser's famous (allegorical) scene of hailing? Is it possible to trace the breakdown of identification? Here I consider the mutually interdependent acts of questioning and confession as a possible instantiation of what Michel

Foucault and Judith Butler have identified as the paradoxical nature of subjection or subjectivation. In dialogue with Franz Kafka's *The Trial*, I return to Arturo Ripstein's *El Santo Oficio*, Sabina Berman's *En el nombre de Dios*, and Jom Tob Azulay's *O Judeu* in order to reflect upon the way in which the modern subject is constituted facing the Law.

THE DISCOURSE OF CONFESSION

When the four limbs had been pulled away, the confessors
came to speak to him; but his executioner told them that he
was dead, though the truth was that I saw the man move, his
lower jaw moving from side to side as if he were talking.
—Michel Foucault

The only thing one has to fear from the excuse is that it will
indeed exculpate the confessor, thus making the confession
(and the confessional text) redundant.
—Paul de Man

The confession possesses a rich and complex history, at once religious, legal, literary, and, as Peter Brooks has demonstrated, psychoanalytic and popular (the last two of which can be witnessed in the contemporary proliferation not only of the "private" practice of psychotherapy but also the very "public" display of selves on talk shows and reality TV programs and, we can now add, social networking sites such as Facebook, Twitter, and Instagram).[1] In his book *Troubling Confessions*, Brooks highlights the distinction between legal and religious confession: while the legal has as its ostensible objective the control of wrongdoing, the religious appears to remain focused on rituals of purification and solace. The fact that the Catholic requirement of confession originates at the very same moment as the birth of the Inquisition in 1215, however, reveals an intrinsic connection between the policing and consolation of the subject, and the subsequent blurring of the bounds between legal and religious confession, between "moral cleansing and moral discipline" (Brooks, *Troubling Confessions*, 2). It is for this reason that I want to consider the history of confession—a unique phenomenon that travels between disparate spaces, both individual and collective—as intimately tied to the modern practice of interrogation.

Brooks explains that the birth of the modern subject, particularly in the romantic era, coincides with the understanding of confession as the means by which the individual articulates (and validates) his inner truth (*Troubling Confessions,* 4). One of the most prominent literary examples of this phenomenon can be discerned within the genre of autobiography, which overlaps in many ways with the discourse of confession, so that we might understand Saint Augustine's spiritual autobiography as a precursor to Jean-Jacques Rousseau's secular *Confessions,* as does J. M. Coetzee in his 1985 essay, "Confession and Double Thoughts." The marriage of autobiography and confession reveals the fact that confession serves not simply as a narration of the self but, more precisely, as an egocentric discourse that posits the self as the center of the textual universe of meaning in which the other is partially or fully eclipsed.[2]

It is through the literary that we can begin to unpack the act of confession, not only because literature exposes the creative or performative qualities of the confession, but also because literary criticism can potentially point to multiple layers of motives and desires that mask, substitute, or compensate for the presence of "authenticity" or lack thereof in the subject and her confession. Reflecting upon Saint Augustine's admission that, as a boy, he had stolen pears from his neighbors not in order to eat them, but rather for the sheer pleasure of committing an act that was forbidden, Coetzee argues that "[Augustine's] story of the pears is . . . a twofold confession of something he knows (the act) and something he does not know: 'I would . . . confess what I know about myself; I will confess what I do not know about myself . . . What I do not know about myself I will continue not to know until the time when 'my darkness is as the noonday' in thy sight' " ("Confession and Double Thoughts," 252). Coetzee's reading underscores a central trait of the confessional genre that allows us to understand the way in which interrogation, too, is motivated by the disquiet surrounding the not-known of the self or the other.[3]

Because the marrano is always already represented as a subject that guards an unreadable secret, the notion that confession responds to that which cannot be known about the self sheds crucial light upon marrano interrogation and confession. Conversely, situating marrano interrogation and confession within the broader tradition of autobiographical confession indicates that the modern subject, too, conceals something fundamentally unknowable: a secret that, returning to Derrida, exceeds the play of both hiddenness *and* revelation. If, as Ricardo Forster has argued, the marrano represents a fault line within the modern subject, both historically and symbolically, interrogation and confession become vital acts through which the Inquisition attempts to purify or make

whole this fragmented subject, the core of which is marked by a breach
or fissure. The New Christian as guilty subject—a subject "at fault"—is
a productive concept that exposes the fault line within the Old Christian subject, as well as the process whereby this fault is inscribed upon
the body of the marrano. Perhaps, then, it makes more sense to speak
not of historical marranos—that is, of the Jews who converted to Catholicism and their descendants—but rather of the *subject as marrano*, a
crypto-subject that guards, always and in every case, an illegible secret.
This is of course what Derrida aims to underscore in his characteriza-
tion of the "universal Marrano" as "anyone who remains faithful to a
secret that he has not chosen."[4]

How is the "not-known" represented, how does it enter the order
of representation? Because it is precisely the unreadability of the truth
of the other that provokes interrogation in the first place, because the
desire for confession (of the self, of the other) can be read as the desire
to access the secret of the other and (finally) because it is the *impossibility* of this access that fuels Inquisitional violence (and preserves desire),
we are confronted here with a problem that is at once ethical, political,
and aesthetic. The question of the representation of the other (or of the
other within the same) is therefore central to our discussion of questioning and confession. From this vantage point, the *content* of the confession is largely irrelevant: it is rather the *act* of confessing that serves to
erase or camouflage the unease related to the enigma of the other.

Challenging the conventional focus on the constative or cognitive
elements of the confession, Paul de Man highlights the performative
quality of confessional discourse in his reading of Rousseau by turning
to the literary in order to underscore the competing motives and desires
that drive confession. One of the early and, at least on the surface, triv-
ial "crimes" admitted to by Rousseau is the theft of a "pink and silver
colored ribbon" while working as a servant to an aristocratic family in
Turin. When confronted by his employer, Rousseau denies any involvement in the crime, blaming the robbery on another servant, Marion,
who, he claims, has absconded with it with the intention of giving it
to Rousseau. Confessing to the reader that this false accusation is far
worse than the theft itself, he explains that Marion's name came to
mind because he secretly harbored romantic feelings for her, that is,
his desire for the ribbon masked a deeper desire for his coworker. But
if Rousseau offers the reader a ready-made interpretation of his inner
world, de Man's analysis of this scene suggests another, unexpected fac-
tor motivating Rousseau's profession of guilt: "What Rousseau *really*

wanted is neither the ribbon nor Marion, but the public scene of exposure which he actually gets. . . . The more crime there is, the more theft,
lie, slander, and stubborn persistence in each of them, the better. The
more there is to expose, the more there is to be ashamed of; the more
resistance to exposure, the more satisfying the scene, and, especially, the
more satisfying and eloquent the belated revelation, in the later narrative, or the inability to reveal" (*Allegories of Reading*, 285). De Man's
analysis makes a vital contribution to the discussion of literary confession by demonstrating that it is neither the stolen object *nor* the object
of lust that motivates Rousseau (de Man shows that the latter serves to
explain and thus excuse the former, as if Rousseau's admonishable behavior were forgivable when viewed through the lens of romantic love),
but rather his desire for self-exposure, that is, the desire for the act of
confession. The confession, then, serves as the condition of possibility
for the construction of the narrative subject itself: without the crime,
there is no confession; without the confession, there is no guilt; without
guilt, there is no text.

De Man's critique of Rousseau allows us to see that interrogation
narratives correspond to the broader tradition of the confessional genre
and that while, at first glance, interrogation may be viewed as an opposing or counter-example to confession (simply put, one is voluntary while
the other is coerced), in reality it serves as a parallel case, an analogous
discursive phenomenon that, rather than enacting a reversal, launches
an unexpectedly similar textual process. If Rousseau's *Confessions*, according to de Man, do not affirm the positive or negative status of the
subject's morality, but instead create a space within which the narrative
subject is constituted, a similar dynamic of exposure is at work in the
interrogation that, while the power relations are inverted, allows for
"truth" (read as fiction) to be invented, for the subject to be fashioned
through the performative verbal acts of interrogation and confession. In
aesthetic representations of these acts, a further possibility is introduced:
that of either invalidating the truth-making process of interrogation or,
paradoxically, affirming it despite the contrary moral or ideological position the text may take against the injustice of the act.

Uma Ideia Oculta: *Interiority and Confession*

Bearing in mind the relationship between desire, guilt, and confession—
or, more precisely, the desire *for* guilt and confession that de Man finds
in Rousseau—I would like to turn now to Gonçalves de Magalhães's

O poeta e a inquisição, an interesting case study in that, unlike the majority of Inquisition narratives analyzed in this book, interrogation and torture remain virtually absent from its pages. In the tragic play, Gonçalves de Magalhães imagines Antônio José da Silva as an innocent New Christian whom the Inquisition authorities have falsely accused. Although his mother converted from Judaism to Christianity, so that his blood is irreversibly tainted, the play does not depict the protagonist himself as practicing Judaism clandestinely. The Inquisition pursues him for reasons that appear beyond or beneath the surface or action: his "Jewishness"—if one can claim that it exists at all—can be found only in the deep recesses of his soul. It is characterized as *uma ideia oculta* that, while revealing a relationship between interiority and subjectivity, absolves the protagonist of any conscious wrongdoing while preserving a traumatic kernel of guilt lodged in the hidden depths of the tragic hero. In what follows, I sustain that rather than dramatizing the traditional scene of marrano interrogation, Magalhães displaces the protagonist's guilt onto Frei Gil who, upon admitting his own transgressions, reinforces the conventional link between confession and truth, preserving the function of Catholic confession as both cathartic and redemptive.

The play's ostensible defense of Antônio José's innocence is communicated through the protagonist's own ideas of truth, which he articulates in response to his persecution by the Inquisition. Reflecting upon the corrupt nation he inhabits, he recites a poetic manifesto of sorts, in which he rails against the assault by the state upon the autonomy of the artist. Rejecting the idea that the poet should propagate falsehood, Antônio's monologue situates the artist in a privileged locus of enunciation, depicting him as guardian of the truth:

> Que quereis afinal? Que o vate seja
> Poeta cortesão? Que se mascare?
> Que nunca diga as coisas claramente?
> Que combine a verdade com a mentira? . . .
> Poeta que calcula quando escreve,
> Que lima quando diz, porque não fira,
> Que procura aradar a todo mundo,
> Que, medroso, não quer aventurar-se,
> Que vá poetisar para os conventos.
> Eu gosto dos Poetas destemidos,
> Que dizem as verdades sem rebuço,
> Que a lira não profanam, nem se vendem;

Estes sim, são Poetas. (Gonçalves de Magalhães, *O poeta e a inquisição*, 30–31)

What do you want in the end? That the bard should be
A courtly poet? That he should wear a disguise?
That he should never say things clearly?
That he should mix truth with lie? . . .
A poet who calculates when he writes,
Who polishes when he speaks, so that he doesn't cause harm,
Who seeks to please everyone,
Who, afraid, refuses to take risks,
He should go recite poetry for the nuns.
I prefer courageous poets,
That speak truths without fear,
That do not profane the verse, that do not sell out;
They are true poets.

The naïve assumption that the poet can express an authentic, transcendent truth, if he so desires, that truth is something that exists and can be expressed through language at will, is symptomatic of the universe of meaning within which the play operates. First, the poet's monologue establishes a clear distinction between truth and falsehood. Second, it relies upon a transparency of language that would make the "truth" representable. Third, it suggests that the autonomous subject can decide, through free will, to tell the truth or to lie. Finally, it grants the artist a privileged position from which to express this truth, rejecting the idea of a crypto-poet who would don a disguise, thus circumventing his obligation to this truth.

Poetry can therefore itself be read as a sort of confession in Magalhães: an ostensibly authentic genre employed in the (profoundly moral or moralizing) service of a transcendent value. This move grants Antônio José a privileged position within the moral landscape of the play: the public is meant to take everything he says at face value, to view him as a bearer of the truth. Curiously, however, interrogation of the New Christian victim is virtually absent from *O poeta e a Inquisição*. When Antônio *does* confess, he does so before friends and of his own free will, rather than under duress to the authorities. His is a confession that, perhaps counterintuitively, seeks to prove innocence through the language of guilt:

E por que causa?
Por uma opinião, por uma idéia
Que minha mãe herdou de seus maiores,
E a transmitiu ao filho!—E sou culpado!

. . .

Por uma idéia oculta de minha alma?
Por que em vez de seguir a lei de Cristo,
Sigo a Lei de Moysés! (Gonçalves de Magalhães, O *poeta e a*
   inquisição, 52)

And for what reason?
For an opinion, for an idea
That my mother inherited from her elders,
And transmitted to her son!—I am accused!

. . .

For a hidden idea in my soul?
Because instead of following the law of Christ,
I follow the Law of Moses!

Here, Antônio describes a guilt that is superficial, unfounded, and at the same time intrinsic to his very being. On the one hand, his confession betrays a constitutive guilt, an unavoidable trace of transgression that he cannot escape.[5] He appears to admit that he follows Judaic law, despite the fact that the play never depicts him observing a single Jewish rite. At the same time, it makes light of this guilt, ridiculing the power that would seek to prosecute him on such shaky grounds.

It is not until we arrive at the figure of Frei Gil, the priest whose declared mission is the salvation of Antônio José's companion, Mariana, that the deeply Catholic nature of the play's vision of the relationship between guilt and confession becomes apparent. After relentlessly pursuing the young woman under the guise of saving her soul, Frei Gil admits that he harbors romantic feelings toward her—what contemporary reader would be shocked by this fact?—and that it is transgressive desire that has motivated his pursuit of the innocent woman. In a kind of perverse variation on his own religious tradition, the priest tells Mariana that he would like to speak to her alone, without witnesses: "vos quero falar sem testemunha" (Gonçalves de Magalhães, O *poeta e a inquisição,* 41). We know from de Man that "vos quero" is inseparable from "vos quero falar": the priest's desire for Mariana is rooted in his desire to confess his *segredo*, his secret—itself a reference to the crypto-Jew's *ideia oculta*—rather than the other way around. Before Gil reveals his secret to Mariana, however, he drives her to acknowledge her own regret, to which he responds by simultaneously rejoicing and begging forgiveness himself:

> Estais arrependida!—Oh que alegria
> Me banha o coração! Minha alma voa;
> Nem posso sustentar-me. Oh se soubesses
> Que prazer me causais neste momento!
> Eu tudo vos perdôo; e me arrependo
> De vos haver tratado com dureza.
> Perdoai-me também; vós perdoais-me? (*Como ajoelhando-se, mas não de todo.*)
> Não é assim? Dizei. De vossos lábios
> Quero ouvir meu perdão; essa voz doce,
> Que me faz palpitar de amor o peito.
> Vinde, cara Mariana; eu vos adoro.
> Abraçai-me. (Gonçalves de Magalhães, O *poeta e a inquisição*, 45–46)

> You are repentant!—Oh what joy
> Bathes my heart! My soul soars;
> I can barely contain myself. If only you knew
> What pleasure you give me this moment!
> I forgive you everything; and I repent
> For having treated you harshly.
> Forgive me as well; do you forgive me? (*As if kneeling, but not completely.*)
> Is it so? Speak. From your lips
> I want to hear my pardon; that sweet voice,
> That causes my heart to palpitate in my chest.
> Come, dear Mariana; I adore you.
> Embrace me.

In Frei Gil's confessional monologue—the first of two—it becomes clear that what Gil desires in Mariana's confession approximates that which he desires in his own. It is the confession itself, the language of the erotic as well as the language of guilt, that stands as the object of desire. A circular logic or structure governs the confession: desire produces guilt, which in turn produces confession (which produces desire, which produces guilt, and so on). In this scene, the confession produces even more guilt, as Frei Gil's secret sends Mariana into such an extreme state of horror that she eventually dies—a result, we are led to believe, of exposure to the monster the priest has revealed himself to be.

Following Mariana's death, a second confession takes place, in which Frei Gil makes Antônio José his interlocutor, reversing the roles of confessant and confessor. Ignorant of Frei Gil's double crime—desire and murder—Antônio asks the priest, "Quem sois vós?", by which he means, who are you (to need to confess to me)? (Gonçalves de Magalhães, *O poeta e a inquisição*, 57). Gil responds:

> Um perverso, um criminoso
> Diante do Senhor, e ante meus olhos,
> E indigno do perdão que ouso implorar-vos.
> Eu perturbei a vossa paz terrestre;
> Arranquei-vos do mundo, e sepultei-vos
> Nesta escura masmorra . . . assassinei-vos!
> Fui eu . . . Que horror! . . . Eu mesmo. Oh, Mariana! (Gonçalves de
>   Magalhães, *O poeta e a inquisição*, 57)

> A pervert, a criminal
> Before the Lord, and before my own eyes,
> And undeserving of the pardon I beg of you.
> I disturbed your earthly peace;
> I uprooted you from the world, and buried you
> In this dark dungeon . . . I murdered you!
> It was I . . . What horror! . . . It was I. Oh, Mariana!

The slippage between addressees—Frei Gil speaks at once to Antônio José, whom he faces, and to Mariana, who is gone—implies that in addition to begging Mariana's forgiveness, he also seeks Antônio José's pardon.

The final lines of the priest's confession, while delivered in the presence of Antônio José, are directed to God. This cathartic moment—"Oh Providência! Em núncio de desgraças me convertes!" ("Oh Providence! You convert me into an apostle of disgrace!") (61)—cements the relationship between the church and salvation, which necessarily takes place through the act of confession. Here, the void created by the absence of Inquisitorial interrogation is filled by the confession of the perverse priest. Rather than the typical interrogation and confession of the New Christian we see in other Inquisition dramas, here we have an alternative guilty subject, a foil of sorts: the priest, who metonymically represents the church itself. The effect of this transference is twofold. First, it establishes a link between confession and conversion, which then must be read through the figure of the crypto-Jew: Inquisitorial confession, the play insinuates, completes the imperfect process of transformation from Jew to Christian. In this sense, while the play appears on the surface to cast blame upon the church (the desiring priest is guilty, the New Christian poet innocent), in reality it preserves the logic of the Inquisition by maintaining the bond between confession (specifically, the confession of guilt, of truth) and conversion. Second, it exposes the relationship between desire and guilt: the guilty subject is guilty, ultimately, for having desired, but the subject also *necessarily desires guilt* and therefore confesses not to excuse himself but to ensure his very guilt, to preserve desire. It is within the latter that we can locate a potential for resistance to Inquisitional logic, even if it is not realized fully within the play itself. As I will suggest in the following section, it is desire that gestures toward the gap between the Real and its symbolization, so that if the aesthetic work succeeds in exposing this gap, it can offer—at least in theory—a possible avenue of resistance to the Law.

BEFORE THE LAW

I love you, gentlest law, through which we yet
were ripening while with it we contended . . .
—Rainer Maria Rilke

"The court has a strange attraction, doesn't it?"
—F. Bürstner, in Franz Kafka, *The Trial*

In order to account sufficiently for distinct practices of confession—whether religious, literary, legal, psychotherapeutic, or otherwise—it becomes necessary to turn to the question that provokes such a declaration from the subject.[6] Within the context of police interrogation, this question is overt, pronounced by those in power. Yet even when there is no explicit question, as in autobiography, the confession responds to an implied question, the question of the big Other to which Slavoj Žižek refers in this chapter's epigraph. Citing Jacques-Alain Miller,

Žižek states that "the subject is not a question, it is as an answer, the answer of the Real to the question asked by the big Other, the symbolic order.... It is not the subject which is asking the question; the subject is the void of the impossibility of answering the question of the Other" (Žižek, *Sublime Object*, 178). The big Other does not have to be external, of course: since the Other can reside within the deepest recesses of the subject, the question is not so much implicit as it is always already posed. In this sense the subject can be understood as constituted through the act of responding to the question of the Other. The subject's response—the confession—is thus constitutive of the subject even as it marks its limit or impossibility, because of the ultimate inability to properly answer the question. It is the impropriety of confession, the impossibility of representing an authentic "self," that I hope to emphasize in the following analysis of literary scenes of interrogation as interpellation.

Interpellation and Guilt

Toward the end of Franz Kafka's *The Trial,* Josef K., who has suffered the persecution of the Law throughout the arduous narrative, finds himself in a cathedral. His boss at the bank has called him there under the pretext of meeting an Italian client who wants to tour the city, but when he arrives, the protagonist encounters an abandoned sanctuary. In lieu of a congregation, he sees vacant pews; rather than meeting a client, he finds himself alone, save for a lone elderly woman kneeling before a portrait of the Virgin. Suddenly, a priest appears behind the podium as if poised to deliver a sermon. Instead of preaching to a community of churchgoers, however, he addresses only the protagonist, bellowing "Josef K.!" (Kafka, *The Trial,* 211). This climactic scene can be read as symptomatic of the broader dynamic of accusation and guilt in the work as a whole: in place of the various agents of the Law who have pursued Josef, despite his alleged innocence, this time a representative of the church issues a call to which the protagonist has no choice but to respond, but which right away incriminates him. "If he turned around he was caught," the narrator explains, "for then he would have confessed that he understood quite well, that he really was the person named, and that he was prepared to obey" (211).

Of course Josef K. *does* turn, though it can't quite be claimed that he understands anything beyond the fact that he must turn, which has been interpreted by critics like Žižek as an instantiation of Althusserian interpellation. As we know from his famous essay "Ideology and Ideological State Apparatuses," Louis Althusser defines ideological interpellation as the process by which the modern subject is formed: "Ideology 'acts' or 'functions' in such a way that it 'recruits' subjects among the individuals (it recruits them all), or 'transforms' the individuals into subjects (it transforms them all) by that very precise operation which I have called *interpellation* or hailing, and which can be imagined along the lines of the most commonplace everyday police (or other) hailing: 'Hey, you there!' . . . The hailed individual will turn around. By this mere one-hundred-and-eighty-degree physical conversion, he becomes a *subject*. Why? Because he has recognized that the hail was 'really' addressed to him, and that 'it was *really him* who was hailed' (and not someone else)" (Althusser, "Ideology," 174). In turning to face the priest, Josef K. hopes to achieve what he has sought throughout his travails: his own constitution as a subject through his insertion in the symbolic order, that is, the recognition that there exists a "really him" that *can* be hailed.[7] The vital role that desire plays in the turning of the subject toward the Law has been detailed by Judith Butler, who defines subjection as "the process of becoming subordinated by power as well as the process of becoming a subject," explaining that "whether by interpellation, in Althusser's sense, or by discursive productivity, in Foucault's, the subject is initiated through a primary submission to power" (*Psychic Life of Power*, 2). It is the subject's passionate attachment to those upon whom she depends that produces the paradoxical desire for subjection: Butler tells us that the subject "would rather exist in subordination than not exist" at all (7).

The difference between Kafka's scene "In the Cathedral" and Althusser's allegorical example of the police officer hailing the citizen is that in Kafka, the call of the Other (the Law) is empty. Žižek claims that the priest's hailing of Josef K. represents "an *interpellation without identification/subjectivation;* it does not offer us a Cause with which to identify—the Kafkaesque subject is the subject desperately seeking a trait with which to identify, he does not understand the meaning of the call of the Other" (Žižek, *Sublime Object*, 44). In Kafka, it is precisely the incomprehensibility of the Law—"the fact that *its authority is without truth*"—that provokes desire in the subject (38). The absent center of the Law, the impossibility of accessing any positive content, is implied from the very beginning of *The Trial*.

Mladen Dolar has followed a similar path in reading Althusser against himself although, unlike Butler and Žižek, both of whom aim to expose the "limits" of interpellation, Dolar strives to recover an aspect of Althusser's work that has been forgotten "in a psychoanalytic sense" (75). According to Dolar, a Lacanian reading of interpellation is already anticipated by the French Marxist philosopher himself. Dolar insists that the apparently sudden transformation of individual into subject *necessarily* produces a remainder, so that "the subject is precisely the failure to become the subject" (77–78). Butler's account of this failure is worded in the following way: "identity can never be fully totalized by the symbolic, for what it fails to order will emerge within the imaginary as a *disorder,* a site where identity is contested" (*Psychic Life of Power,* 97, italics my own). In what follows, I examine three scenes of interrogation (or lack of interrogation) that lead up to the climactic scene in the cathedral as provoked by or responding to the void at the heart of the Law. Departing from the traditional dynamic of question and answer inherent in the act of interrogation, in positing the content of the Law as empty, Kafka highlights the desire of the subject to be interrogated and to confess, because the alternative would signify surrendering existence, conceding the subject's place in the social order.

The novel opens with the following statement by the narrator: "Someone must have slandered Josef K., for one morning, without having done anything wrong, he was arrested" (Kafka, *The Trial,* 3). That the protagonist's blamelessness should initiate the plot is significant, but we must not necessarily take the narrator at his word. If we are to read the declaration of innocence literally, K.'s arrest is simply a case of mistaken identity.[8] Yet as we are to see, the protagonist immediately begins to assume guilt, or perhaps he is already guilty: in Althusserian terms, after all, "they hardly ever miss their man" (174). An individual is always already constituted as a subject; he merely rehearses the rituals of ideological recognition in order to guarantee his concreteness and irreplaceability as a subject. Therefore the entire plot that follows does not so much trace K.'s entrance into the symbolic order as much as it reveals the fact that he is already a part of it. Rather than tracing a chronology or a causality, *The Trial* exposes the role that desire plays in the subject's turn to the call of the Other.

When the inspectors arrive to accuse the protagonist, Josef K. realizes that he shouldn't have spoken to them and that, in doing so, he has justified their reason for being there. By turning toward them (here, a turn realized specifically through language), the protagonist ensures his own bind: by "confessing" his innocence, he instead confirms his guilt. Responding to K.'s insistence that this has all been a terrible mistake, that they have the wrong man, one of the inspectors states that the Law does not err because it is attracted by guilt: "'There's been no mistake. After all, our department, as far as I know, and I know only the lowest level, doesn't seek out guilt among the general population, but, as the Law states, is attracted by guilt and has to send us guards out. That's the Law. What mistake could there be?' 'I don't know that law,' said K. . . . The guard merely said dismissively: 'You'll feel it eventually.' Franz broke in and said: 'You see, Willem, he admits that he doesn't know the Law and yet he claims he's innocent'" (Kafka, *The Trial*, 8–9). The Law, then, is not merely omniscient: it relies upon desire as a kind of compass that points it in the right direction, to draw it to its target, guaranteeing K.'s inevitable inclusion within it.

Kafka depicts his protagonist as equally attracted to his own guilt. The inseparability of desire and guilt becomes more evident in the second chapter, in which K. seeks forgiveness for the guards' intrusion into the room of fellow boarder Fräulein Bürstner. "'Your room was slightly disturbed today, and in a sense it was my fault,'" he confesses to his attractive neighbor. "'It was done by strangers and against my will, and yet, as I say, it was my fault; that's what I wanted to ask your pardon for'" (Kafka, *The Trial*, 28). K. could just as easily have worded his confession as an accusation, fully pinning the blame upon the guards who forcibly entered her room and meddled with her belongings. Instead he phrases it as an admission, as if he *wished* to be blamed for the other's crime. Without entering into a detailed psychoanalytic reading of the scene, K. is on one level confessing his own desire to be in Fräulein Bürstner's room—indeed, his desire to be in Bürstner herself—which is why the scene inevitably ends with a transgressive kiss between the two "guilty" parties (Bürstner, for her part, is guilty of staying out late every night, and being seen with different men in different neighborhoods, raising the suspicion of their landlady Frau Grubach). It is Fräulein Bürstner, finally, who intimates that the Law is not only drawn to the guilty party, but also that, conversely, the subject is always drawn to the Law: "'The court has a strange attraction, doesn't it?'" she asks K. seductively (29).

Just before their kiss, Josef K. relates to F. Bürstner the details of his case, assuring her that, in the end, no inquiry took place. Of course, he is also profoundly disappointed by the lack of questioning, which he continues to pursue for the remainder of the novel, even as he repeatedly proclaims his innocence. In the next chapter, "Initial Inquiry," K. receives a call informing him that an interrogation will take place at the court, a development that appears to inspire relief in the protagonist. Indeed, more than the possibility that the "trial" is a case of mistaken identity, it is the court's failure to live up to K's idea of it that most unnerves him. Unfortunately, the protagonist's first appearance before the court proves even more maddening than his encounter with the guards in his home. The court's absurdity produces outrage in the protagonist, who despairs less because of the fate that awaits him than because of the utter senselessness of the Law.

To begin with, the examining magistrate immediately accuses him of having arrived late, despite the fact that he was never told when to appear. When the court officials refuse to interrogate him—the only question posed to Josef K. is "You're a house painter?" (44), betraying once again a constitutive *misrecognition* at the heart of his encounter with the Law—he offers his own public statement to the court. His speech goes on for nearly six pages, during which time he does not so much defend himself (what one might expect of a defendant in a typical legal proceeding), but rather addresses the process to which he has been submitted, and to which he believes others have been submitted as well.[9] The protagonist's unwillingness to acknowledge either his guilt or innocence, of course, is logical: in the most literal reading of the events that make up his trial, he has never been accused of a crime, and thus finds it difficult to mount a proper defense. What the scene tells us figuratively, however, is that the trial cannot be reduced to a mere establishment of guilt or innocence of a specific crime. The novel's title in German, *Der Prozeß*, suggests that what is at stake here is much more than a simple courtroom trial with a beginning, middle, and end. Instead, the "process" includes the numerous proceedings, investigations, and questionings that take place throughout the course of the novel, as well as the more existential, internal, ceaseless ordeal endured by the protagonist.

K.'s monologue, which is met alternatively with silence from the magistrate and uproarious laughter and applause from the public, is exposed as an ultimately futile attempt to assume some degree of agency in the process, so that when he attempts to "authorize" the magistrate to give secret signals to the public, he appears at once paranoid and powerless. Despite the fact that the court never interrogates the protagonist, together with the fact that his speech is met with an absurd mix of support and ridicule, the monologue is nevertheless crucial, for it is the *absence* of questioning that ultimately creates the space within which Josef K. can protest the proceedings: the empty space left by the absence of questioning paradoxically allows K. to affirm his existence as a subject before the Law.

The final instance of questioning that I would like to explore is the aforementioned scene in the cathedral, in which Josef K. learns that everything belongs to the court. He has, of course, already received clues to this effect, particularly in his interactions with his lawyer and Titorelli the painter, both of whom belong to the court themselves. Many scenes in the novel (represented beautifully in Orson Welles's cinematic version of the work) take place in claustrophic or labyrinthine spaces, all of which end up depositing the protagonist at the courtroom. Each of these sites, in addition to bearing a convoluted architectural form, tends to be inhabited or guarded by a feminine figure: the washerwoman, the lawyer's nurse Leni, and the vermin-like girls who infest Titorelli's attic studio. The women and girls—who inspire attraction as much as repulsion, but who in every case arouse a sense of inescapability in the protagonist—metonymically represent the closed system of the court. Both architecture and feminine sexuality invoke in the reader (and in the viewer of Welles's film) an awareness of the inevitability of K.'s condition, a sense that there is no outside to the Law.

Yet this radical inclusion entails a necessary exclusion: the barring of the subject from the "content" of the Law, a double bind I want to pursue in my readings of Inquisitorial scenes of interrogation below. The parable "Before the Law," related by the priest immediately following his hailing of Josef K., allegorizes this bind.[10] In the tale, a man comes from the country to appear before a portal that guards the Law within its gates. A doorkeeper stands outside in order to prevent the entrance of the man, who then spends the rest of his life waiting, hoping to gain permission to enter. The doorkeeper allows the man from the country to wait, even providing a stool to ease his discomfort. He accepts all bribes the man offers so that he won't feel as if he's neglected anything. The years pass, the man grows old. At the end of his life, the gatekeeper reveals to the man: "'No one else could gain admittance here, because this entrance was meant solely for you. I'm going to go and shut it now'" (Kafka, *The Trial*, 217). The aporetic nature of the Law (the gate is destined for nobody but you, and now I must close it) has been read by Žižek as that which ensures the subject's attraction to the Law while guaranteeing his subjectivation: "The process of interpellation-subjectivation is precisely an attempt to elude, to avoid this traumatic kernel through identification," he argues, explaining that "in assuming a symbolic mandate, in recognizing himself in the interpellation, the subject evades the dimension of the Thing" (*Sublime Object*, 181). The stubborn gap between identification and the traumatic kernel that resists it, between the Real and its symbolization, ensures desire for the Law—or for identification with the Law—while creating the conditions of possibility of resistance to such identification, that which Judith Butler denominates "refused identification" (*Psychic Life of Power*, 132).[11] In what follows, I explore the way this double bind signals a limit to the totality of the Law while allowing for a remainder that cannot be fully incorporated or totalized.

The Marrano as Subject-at-Fault

The double bind of subjection and subjectivation is, as we know from Foucault, decidedly modern. How does the figure of the marrano, which from its inception marks the impossibility of the autonomous Cartesian subject, allow us to understand this phenomenon more clearly? More specifically, how is the dilemma of the modern subject played out through the interrogated marrano, and to what degree can we understand this condition as desired or desirable, especially when we consider that, historically, the marrano was largely a forced socio-religious identitary category? Finally, why is it in the space of the aesthetic that these questions can be articulated best, or uniquely?

In *Literature and Subjection*, Horacio Legrás sustains that "the aesthetic dimension embodies better than any other the specifically modern type of subjection" (84). He claims that this is so, following Jürgen Habermas, because it is the work of art that best represesents "the question of autonomous immanence" (85). If the work of art instantiates the autonomy celebrated within modernity, and if the marrano exposes its impossibility, what happens within the work of art that seeks to represent the marrano as guilty subject, as a subjected being? In my reading of aesthetic scenes of Inquisitorial interrogation in Ripstein, Berman, and Azulay, I argue that the work of art walks a line (indeed, as does the marrano) between autonomy and subjection, between the articulation of Inquisitional logic and a logic that would subvert totalitarian or totalizing thought. The line walked by the aesthetic (and by the marrano) can be read as a fault line: one that marks a breach within the modern subject and that constitutes this subject as always already at fault. Legrás gestures in a similar direction when he outlines the paradoxical negation of modern subjectivity by art: "the project of aesthetic self-foundation that was supposed to bring to completion the enlightened ideal of a rational grounding of the self is threatened rather than confirmed by the collusion of modern subjectivity and art" (85). It is therefore within the realm of the aesthetic that we can begin to unpack the aporetic nature of the interrogated marrano as a guilty subject, or a subject "at fault."

In my discussion of *marranismo* in chapter 1, I describe the way in which two competing spaces are delineated in Ripstein's *El Santo Oficio:* one private (crypto-Jewish) and the other public (Catholic). The marrano traverses these divided spheres, which are structured around a central antagonism between New Christian and Old and, in the film, nearly every "encounter" between the two worlds rehearses distinct forms of questioning or interpellation. In one of the earliest scenes of *El Santo Oficio*, the protagonist Luis de Carvajal and his brother Baltasar are depicted walking on a deserted road outside town, when two monks suddenly appear and ask the brothers to identify themselves—"¿Son criollos?"—to which Luis and Baltasar respond, "Peninsulares" (19). That the very first words uttered by the men concern the question of identity demonstrates the extremely quotidian way in which interpellation takes place. These scenes of hailing can occur outside spaces explicitly identifiable as belonging to the Law or the State (the courtroom, the torture chamber, etc.), which is why Žižek claims that one "need not refer to such exemplary cases as police interrogation or religious confession" to understand that "questioning is the basic procedure of the totalitarian intersubjective relationship" (*Sublime Object,* 179). Once the Carvajal brothers have identified themselves—if not as Europeans born in New Spain, then at least as their ethnic counterparts from across the Atlantic—the monks warn them of an epidemic, "Hay epidemia: dicen que los judíos están envenenando los pozos" (Ripstein and Pacheco, *El Santo Oficio,* 19). The scene of interpellation-identification is cemented with an indirect accusation of guilt: the monks have indeed found their men, even if they do not know it. The formal and informal scenes of questioning that follow in *El Santo Oficio* work to constitute the crypto-Jew as a guilty subject, while cementing the bond between torture and truth.

The dynamic of questioning at the heart of totalitarian power is rehearsed within official interrogation spaces as well as the unofficial site of the "street," establishing guilt as a sort of psychic anchor that tethers the subject to power. Terror and torture are central to the "softening" of the crypto-Jewish subject to be questioned: after the Carvajal family has been incarcerated, the guards undress, rape, and beat Luis's mother,

Francisca, and sister, Mariana. The screenplay depicts the rape of Mariana in the following way: "El primero se aproxima, la toma por el talle y con una mano le cierra la boca. Mariana se estremece en el paroxismo del terror. El segundo ayudante la doblega y empieza a desnudarla" ("The first approaches her, grabs her clothing and with one hand covers her mouth. Mariana trembles in a fit of terror. The second attendant bends her over and begins to undress her") (Ripstein and Pacheco, *El Santo Oficio*, 47). These methods of torture were typical not only of Inquisitorial procedures, but can also be found in current practices of imprisonment and abuse. One need not look further than the photographs of Abu Ghraib to learn that forced nudity itself—preceding or in place of more extreme sexual abuse such as rape—serves as a common psychological technique employed to dismantle (or "unmake," in Elaine Scarry's terms) the prisoner's identity and, I would add, in order to "remake" or reconstitute the prisoner as guilty subject, as a subject "at fault." Francisca herself protests that "no hay mayor tormento que verme desnuda y afrentada" ("there is no greater torture than to look at me naked and humiliated") (53). The interrogation of Mariana and Francisca is accompanied by the official's disclaimer (which echoes those found in historical Inquisition documents) that the responsibility for the torture lies with the victim, rather than the torturer: "si en dicho tormento muriera o fuese lisiada, sea a su culpa y cargo y no a la nuestra, por no haber querido decir la verdad" ("if in said torture you are to die or are to be injured, it is of your own fault and responsibility and not ours, for refusing to tell the truth") (51). This statement assures that the prisoner is always already guilty: guilty of heresy, but also guilty of the very violence about to be committed by the torturer.

The effects of this unmaking and remaking, moreover, are not limited to the prisoner whose body is violated. In Ripstein, Mariana's rape is heard by the rest of the family and adds to their torment as well. As the screams of his mother echo throughout the prison, Luis cries out "Madre, madre, madre . . . No . . ." until a guard arrives to silence him (Ripstein and Pacheco, *El Santo Oficio*, 46). Even Frey Gaspar, the Catholic (and therefore "innocent") brother who has denounced them, does not escape unscathed: it is reported that "se quedó mudo cuando encarcelaron a su familia" ("he became mute when they arrested his family") (41). Fully aware of the fate he has brought upon his family, Gaspar joins them in their suffering, and eventually perishes as well.

In the torture of Luis, the questioning is repetitive, one might say redundant, highlighting the way in which we "constantly practice the rituals of ideological recognition" (Althusser, "Ideology," 172–73). During his initial arrest and interrogation, Luis renounces his heresy in order to free himself, despite the fact that he has become *more* Jewish while in jail, as I detail in chapter 1. The second time he is tied to the rack, he confesses all the names of his fellow Judaizers, even though he has sworn to the community that he will invent false information to spare their lives.

Peralta: Di la verdad.

Guerrero: Primera vuelta.

Hacen girar los cordeles. Luis grita de dolor.

Luis: Es cierto que mi madre, mi hermana y yo abjuramos en falso y nunca hemos dejado de creer en la Santa Ley que Dios entregó a Moisés en la cumbre del Sinaí.

. . .

Guerrero: Tercera vuelta.

Accionan otra vez el potro. El aullido de Luis se hace aun más doloroso.

. . .

Luis: También el doctor Morales y su hija Catalina y Justa Méndez . . .

. . .

Guerrero: Sexta vuelta.

Los cordeles del potro se hunden nuevamente en la carne de Luis.

. . .

Luis: Y guardan la ley de Moisés: Gregorio López, Miguel de Lucena, Juan de Almeyda, Constanza Rodríguez, Clara Henríquez, Sebastián de la Peña, Tomás Cardozo, Antonio Díaz Márquez y Beatriz, su mujer; Cristóbal Gómez, Ana Zúñiga y su hijo Carlos, Elena Báez . . . (Ripstein and Pacheco, *El Santo Oficio*, 91–95)

Peralta: Tell the truth.

Guerrero: First turn.

They rotate the cords. Luis screams in pain.

Luis: It is true that my mother, my sister and I gave false testimony and that we have never stopped believing in the Holy Law that God gave Moses at the peak of Sinai.

. . .

Guerrero: Third turn.

The roller is once again activated. Luis's cry becomes even more agonizing.

. . .

Luis: Also Doctor Morales and his daughter Catalina and Justa Méndez . . .

. . .

Guerrero: Sixth turn.

The ropes of the device dig once again into the flesh of Luis.

. . .

Luis: . . . Gregorio López, Miguel de Lucena, Juan de Almeyda, Constanza Rodríguez, Clara Henríquez, Sebastián de la Peña, Tomás Cardozo, Antonio Díaz Márquez y Beatriz, su mujer; Cristóbal Gómez, Ana Zúñiga y su hijo Carlos, Elena Báez . . .

Reading the above scene of interrogation, we can begin to understand how it is that torture works: how the subject is constituted as guilty, how this constitutive guilt precedes the arrest or, more precisely, transcends any kind of temporal causality. At the same time, the film does little to dismantle what Page duBois calls the relationship between torture and truth: under the pain of the torture instrument, Luis confesses what we understand to be an incontestable truth, rather than inventing lies. Yet these two options (truth-telling, lying) are in fact opposite sides of the same coin: whether or not the application of pain elicits a "true" confession, it guarantees torture as the act by which certain truths become and remain legitimate. Here, the truth of identity is never called into question: one is either a believing Christian or a crypto-Jew.

At the same time, the film does hint at another motivation for the torture, a hidden "truth" of the Inquisition. Complementing the rather simplistic scenes of interrogation, in which prisoners may or may not admit guilt, but in which a confession (whether true or false) is produced in nearly every case, are the repressed scenes of unspeakability to which I refer in the previous chapter. First, Mariana is said to go insane following her arrest and torture, which could suggest the possibility of a third term between truth and lie, or truth-telling and lying. Further, the "silences" narrated in the screenplay and portrayed visually in the film (Fray Gaspar's speechlessness, the Indian and mestizo peasants' "unspeakable" poverty, the mute indigenous men) allude to a truth that cannot be articulated through language, specifically through the language of confession.

These silences are broken toward the end of the film by an alternate reading of the "truth" of the Inquisition, the assertion that the actual motive behind the persecution of crypto-Jews in New Spain is not religious but economic: "No le importa salvar las almas sino quedarse con los haberes" ("They care less about saving souls than about garnering their riches") (Ripstein and Pacheco, El Santo Oficio, 97). It is here, in the Marxist subtext of the film, that the dominant message becomes apparent: as I have argued in my discussion of Ripstein's use of allegory, it is not "really" the religious persecution of crypto-Jews that serves as the principal concern of the film, but the ethnic and economic injustices that have their foundation in the colonial period and continue to the present day. The limitations of this move—however potent—have to do with the way in which the void signaled by the mute or the unsayable is filled with political content. El Santo Oficio briefly opens an (ethical) space that would resist Inquisitional logic, and then proceeds to close it through the ideological.

It seems that Luis desires to confess under interrogation, not unlike Rousseau or Josef K. He turns in response to the hailing of the Inquisitor because, while it constitutes him as (always already) guilty, it also preserves his place within the social order. His specific place, of course, is that of the condemned Judaizer, but that is precisely who he wants to be: after repeatedly oscillating between renouncing and assuming Judaism, he utters a final cry ("Shemá . . .") before dying so that, even in death, his status as a Jew is guaranteed. Of course, it is his marranismo that ensures that confession can produce a (guilty) identity; only the "unburied truth" (to return to duBois's account of torture in Athenian culture) of confessed crypto-Jewishness creates the specific conditions for the revelation of truth as alêtheia, or unconcealment. Even an allegorical interpretation, which would project Inquisitional violence onto the broader ethno-political context of colonialism and its aftermath, merely substitutes one truth for another, exposing the reader momentarily to the void of the unsayable but quickly filling it with an ideological "message." Is it possible to imagine an aesthetic work that could approach the political by way of the ethical, that is, that could gesture toward the possible while preserving its unknowability, the impossibility at its core?

Refused Identification

If Ripstein's protagonist desires his own subjection before the Law, Berman's *En el nombre de Dios* pursues an alternate way of conceiving identity and truth in its representation of Inquisitorial violence. On the one hand, as I will demonstrate below, Berman's play can be read as a variation on Kafka's attempt to create a "closed system" in the sense described above. Yet by bringing to the fore the limits of this system, Berman also makes available a realm of potentiality, including potential meaning, beyond the totalizing efforts of the Inquisition. Through the close reading of several scenes of imprisonment, interrogation, and confession, I investigate the way in which Berman problematizes the relationship between subjection and subjectivity, asking whether Butler's notion of "refused identification" is possible within the framework of the theatrical work.

It could be argued that Kafka creates—in *The Trial* as well as *The Castle*—a closed system, a totalizing or total universe. Little by little, Josef K. discovers that everything belongs to the court: his colleagues at the bank, the washerwomen, the Lawyer, Leni, the painter, the vermin-like girls. Architecturally, as well, everything seems to lead to the court: the bank, the cathedral, the painter's studio are all represented as labyrinthine structures that ultimately lead to the courtroom, from which there is no escape. In the second scene of *En el nombre de Dios*, in which Don Luis is questioned by the inquisitors, the stage directions specify that "*Don Luis el Viejo declara ante los inquisidores—no los vemos: en todo caso somos nosotros, el público—*" ("*Don Luis the Elder declares before the Inquisitors—we do not see them: in any case it is us, the public*") (Berman, *En el nombre de Dios*, 331). This move recalls Santareno's attempt to involve the public in the Inquisitional proceedings, in which "[os] espectadores . . . funcionam como assistentes do auto-de-fé" ("the spectators serve as observers of the auto-da-fé") (Santareno, *O Judeu*, 14). Both plays fashion an entire universe out of the stage and audience, implicating the spectator in the violence. Yet a crucial difference exists between these two attempts to create an enclosed universe within the space of the theater. If in Santareno the public appears as potential witnesses, creating the condition of possibility for an ethical demand, in Berman the physical setup interpellates the audience in quite a different way: here, the public occupies the place of the perpetrators of violence, rather than its witnesses. Because the play assumes a critical position against such violence, it is the audience that stands accused: by watching (and therefore "interrogating" Don Luis), the spectator becomes guilty as well.

A prison scene toward the end of *En el nombre de Dios,* following the arrest of Luis the Elder, invokes a similar sensation of total inclusion. Don Luis converses with a fellow prisoner—an old man who recognizes Luis from the bordellos—and the two exchange details about how they have landed in jail. When the guard silences them, the old man asks why *he* is in prison.

> *Soldado:* Por qué estoy en la cárcel? Soy tu carcelero, ¿no ves?
>
> *Viejo (en secreto, al volver a cruzarse con el soldado):* Veo. Pero ¿pero por qué estás en la cárcel, hijo?
>
> *Soldado:* Mira las llaves de tu calabozo: yo soy tu carcelero, ¿no entiendes, viejo loco?
>
> . . .
>
> *Viejo (al cruzarse con Luisito, en secreto):* Pero igual está en la cárcel. (Berman, *En el nombre de Dios,* 375)

> *Guard:* You old imbecile, can't you see my sword, my lance, the keys to your cell on my belt?
>
> *Old Man:* Of course, you're our guard. Excuse me. (*He changes his path.*)
>
> *Guard (laughing to himself):* Why am I in jail? What a question!
>
> . . .
>
> *Old Man:* You're the guard, of course. But you're still in jail. (Berman, *Heresy,* 154)

The scene signals two distinct yet related possibilities. First, the Old Man's reminder that the guard, too, is in jail suggests that the Inquisition is inescapable, that its power reaches even those employed in its service. The second aspect of this dynamic is internal, so that even as the Inquisition's scope is limitless in a spatial sense, the subject can be understood to exist only insofar as he is subjected to the Inquisition. That this bind should apply to the guard as well as to the prisoner suggests that the dilemma of the imprisoned marrano can be translated into a universal: every subject is a marrano insofar as he is subjected to the law of the other, or the other within the same. This is what Judith Butler argues in her psychoanalytic reading of Foucault: "As a form of power, subjection is paradoxical. To be dominated by a power external to one-self is a familiar and agonizing form power takes. To find, however, that what 'one' is, one's very formation as a subject, is in some sense dependent upon that very power is quite another" (*Psychic Life of Power*, 1–2). Butler's reading of power as "psychic" speaks directly to the dilemma dramatized by Berman: power is always already internalized, the subject is by definition subjected, so that subjection even reaches those who occupy positions of power themselves.

In the case of Don Luis, it is the power he has exercised in the colonies as governor and landowner that determines his fate. As his downfall appears increasingly unavoidable, the Governor laments the impossibility of escape from his situation. His desperation confirms the omnipotence of the Inquisition, though it takes on a slightly different tone in this case. Like John Proctor in *The Crucible*, Luis the Elder is concerned above all with the preservation of his name, even as he admits that it is a lost cause. Honor, to the Carvajal patriarch, has less to do with transcendent ideals or morality (as it does for Proctor), and more to do with the question of class or status, so that despite the fact that Felipe Nuñez secures his release from jail and a "temporary" (twenty-year) exile from the Indies, he will be unable to salvage his position within the social order, as Don Luis himself points out: "A uno que sale de la Inquisición no se le permite tener un cargo de gobierno, ni siquiera montar a caballo" ("And my good name? What would happen to my good name? A penitent freed by the Inquisition won't be permitted to wear fine clothing or jewels, not even ride a horse") (155) (376; the English translation teases out the link between honor, status, and the name). This is why, even as Don Luis contemplates suicide, he announces that he has already in a sense died: "Estoy al borde de ya no ser yo" (155) ("I'm on the verge of no longer being me") (376). The "I" that is preemptively mourned in this statement refers to a kind of dethroning of the elite colonial administrator, despite the fact that he was doomed from the beginning due to his impure lineage.

In the end, Don Luis's confession fails to liberate him from his fate; indeed, no one who claims innocence escapes unscathed. The only path to alleged freedom is through the proclamation of guilt: by recanting, repenting, renouncing heresy. One can escape persecution by the system only by subjecting oneself to it, reminiscent of Josef K.'s limited options in Kafka. (We recall that Tintorelli, the court painter, explains to K. that there are only three possible outcomes to his trial—actual acquittal, apparent acquittal, and protraction—but that no one who has been accused has ever managed to secure actual acquittal.) From what, then, does Don Luis escape by taking his own life? If anything, this gesture of apparent agency (he decides his own fate) lands him in an inferior position within the hierarchy of Inquisitorial punishment: instead of being punished with twenty years of exile, his corpse must now be burned at the stake. But if we are to read Don Luis's actions from the vantage point of Josef K.'s trial, perhaps this destiny is preferable to the alternative: complete banishment from the symbolic order, from the universe of sense. By dying within the confines of the Inquisition, Don Luis is able to preserve some form of his identity, even if it is not that of governor.

What, then, might exceed this bleak and totalizing universe? In order to address this question, I want to consider the first scene of the play, which opens as a member of the Carvajal clan is being questioned by Inquisitional authorities.[12] In Berman, the interrogation does not consist of questions about clandestine practices of Judaizing, as was typical of Inquisitional interrogation as well as many of the literary representations of such scenes, but rather revolves around the question of the prisoner's "secret name":

> *Inquisidor:* Tu nombre secreto.
>
> *Hombre:* Hilario de Carbajal.
>
> *Inquisidor:* He dicho: tu nombre secreto.
>
> *Hombre:* . . .
>
> *Inquisidor:* Dénle.
>
> *Azotan al hombre.*
>
> . . .
>
> *Inquisidor:* ¡Tu nombre secreto!
>
> *Verdugo* 1: Pierde el aliento.
>
> *Inquisidor:* ¡Tu nombre secreto!
>
> *Hombre:* Hommm.
>
> *Inquisidor:* ¿Qué qué qué? ¿Qué farfulla?
>
> *Verdugo* 2: Hommm...

Verdugo 1: Hombre ha dicho.

Verdugo 2: ¡Hombre!

Inquisidor: ¡Dice que su nombre secreto es hombre! ¡Ave María Purísima!: no en tinta y papel, sino de carne y hueso, aquí ante nosotros: ¡un pueta [sic]! (*El inquisidor va a sentarse en una esquina. Rutinariamente*) Córtenle la lengua.

Coro: Aaaaaaaaaaaaaaaah! Iiiiiiiiiiiiii!

(*Pausa*)

Inquisidor: Entonces, te preguntaba: ¿tu nombre secreto?

El hombre produce un sonido gutural ininteligible. Risa de los verdugos.

Inquisidor (*suavemente*): Dénle.

Los verdugos alzan los látigos: Oscuro. (Berman, *En el nombre de Dios*, 151–52)

Inquisitor: Your secret name.

Man: Hilario de Carbajal.

Inquisitor: Your secret name, I said.

Man: . . .

Inquisitor: Give it to him.

They whip the man.

. . .

Inquisitor: Your secret name!

First Executioner: He's out of breath.

Inquisitor: Your secret name!

Man: Mmmaann.

First Executioner: What? What? What? What's he jabbering?

Second Executioner: Mmmaann.

First Executioner: Man, he said.

Second Executioner: Man!

Inquisitor: He says his secret name is man! Ave María Purísima! We have before us a poet writing not with pen and paper but with flesh and blood! (*The Inquisitor goes and sits down in a corner. Routinely*) Cut off his tongue.

Chorus: Aaaaaaaaaaaaaaah! Iiiiiiiiiiiii!

(*Pause*)

Inquisitor: Now, I'll ask you again: your secret name?

The man produces an unintelligible guttural sound. The Executioners laugh.

Inquisitor (*gently*): Give it to him.

The Executioners raise their whips: Blackout. (Berman, *Heresy*, 119–20)

Unlike most aesthetic representations of Inquisitional interrogation, Berman's play does not attempt to render an "historically accurate" portrayal of torture—whatever that might mean. Instead, the play employs a highly poetic language and structure in order to perform the gap that lies at the core of the guilty marrano. Berman exposes the fault line that is constitutive of the guilty marrano, the marrano-at-fault, while at the same time signaling that this fault line traverses the subject more universally. Hence the semi-declaration by Hilario that his secret name is "Man," a confession produced through the mouth of the interrogator, performatively revealing the secret of the crypto-Jew as the *lack* of a secret understood as identifiable difference.[13] Instead we are confronted with another class of secret, a failed subject that refuses identification while suggesting an alternative universality in which every subject is pierced by a shard of untranslatability, that which cannot be named or confessed. The torture victim's refusal to reveal a "secret name" (Derrida's *nom propre*) effectively denies that such a name is pronounceable, so that just as the executioners cut off the prisoner's tongue as a way to rob him of his status as speaking subject, the play *itself* violates language as we know it, a conventional or non-literary language, a language that only serves to name the nameable. The "unintelligible guttural sound" that ends the scene articulates the limits of language through the motif of the destroyed tongue. Figurative, or disfigured, language, in Berman, pays homage to Derrida's notion of the secret—not the buried truth of classical torture, but rather a secret that "remains inviolable even when one thinks one has revealed it," a secret that "exceeds the play of veiling/unveiling, dissimulation/revelation, night/day, forgetting/anamnesis, earth/heaven, etc." (Derrida, "Passions," 26).

In denying the conventional notion of torture as that which unearths the truth of the other, Hilario de Carvajal refuses the relationship of interpellation and guilt that Althusser describes. Here, the torture victim can be said to respond, but his response is simultaneously a turning *toward* and a turning *away* from the Law. By violating the "tongue" of the other, the play ultimately forecloses the possibility of the confession of guilt, simultaneously disrupting the theory of the subject grounded in identifiable guilt. Instead, Berman proposes a different kind of subject, a failed subject that exposes the fault line in the modern subject more broadly, a fault line that ultimately stands as the void or the impossibility of the identitary logic that governs modern politics.

It is here that we can begin to imagine what Butler calls "refused identification." In light of what Foucault describes as "the invasion and management of the prisoner's body" (quoted in Butler, *Psychic Life of Power,* 84) through the "signifying practices of the prison [. . . including] confession" (85), Butler turns to the psyche as that which, unlike the subject, "exceeds the imprisoning effects of the discursive demand to inhabit a coherent identity, to become a coherent subject. The psyche is what resists the regularization that Foucault ascribes to normalizing discourses" (86). This is the Lacanian Real for which Althusser's scene of interpellation cannot fully account, according to Dolar (cited in Butler, 122). In contrast to Ripstein's confessing characters, who assume guilt in order to shield themselves from the Real, from the universe of unintelligibility, Berman's Hilario gives way to the Real, a potentially disruptive force that serves as both the motivation for Inquisitorial interrogation as well as its limit.

Hilario's response to the Inquisitor might be understood in terms of Lacan's ethical injunction to not give way on one's desire (*ne pas céder sur son desir*). Žižek reads the Lacanian motto in the following way: "we must not obliterate the distance separating the Real from its symbolization: it is this surplus of the Real over every symbolization that functions as the object-cause of desire. To come to terms with this surplus (or, more precisely, leftover) means to acknowledge a fundamental deadlock ('antagonism'), a kernel resisting symbolic integration-dissolution" (*Sublime Object,* 3). Remaining faithful to one's desire implies not only an ethics of subjectivation, but also a politics of resistance, even at the very place in which one is subjected. Hilario does not quite escape guilt, but instead confronts the impossibility of such escape and refuses its terms.

Torture, Visibility, and Responsibility

I would like to conclude this chapter on figurative representations of marrano interrogation by returning briefly to Azulay's *O Judeu*. In chap-

ter 1, I detail the way in which Azulay establishes an aporetic relationship between spectacle and spectrality, creating a crypto-Jewish subject
that, over and above guarding a secret, exposes the way in which both
New *and* Old Christian subjectivity is performed by oscillating between
the secret and the seen. The most violent aspect of the Inquisition's theatricality, of course, resides in the scenes of interrogation, torture, and
execution of alleged heretics. These spectacles exist in stark contrast
to—yet in their excess paradoxically serve to affirm—the secrecy of the
institution. As Foucault reminds us in *Discipline and Punish,* "public
torture and execution must be spectacular, it must be seen by all almost
as its triumph. The very excess of the violence employed is one of the elements of its glory: the fact that the guilty man should moan and cry out
under the blows is not a shameful side-effect, it is the very ceremonial of
justice being expressed in all its force" (34). Until the eighteenth century,
the excessively public nature of torture and execution accompanied a
highly secretive investigation: "the entire criminal procedure, right up
to the sentence, remained secret: that is to say, opaque, not only to the
public but also to the accused himself" (35). Through the visual genre of
film, Azulay highlights the paradoxically visible and invisible nature of
Inquisitorial torture and castigation described by Foucault, reproducing
the violence of the spectacle while creating the conditions of possibility
for an ethics and politics of witnessing.

Torture in *O Judeu* is represented in a simple, unexaggerated, realist tone; rather than turning to melodrama, Azulay allows the victims'
screams to speak for themselves. This is not to say that these images are
unmediated; on the contrary, there is a strong sense of the gaze in these
scenes. While the first instance of torture highlights the voyeuristic gaze
of a "team" of male torturers and physicians as a naked Leonor hangs
from the ceiling, the dynamic of voyeurism is subtler in the interrogation of Antônio, whose exposed body is only shown from the waist
up.[14] (The sexualization of torture is not unrelated to the gendering of
guilt in the film: only women are seen observing or espousing the beliefs
and practices of Judaism, while the male protagonist is portrayed as a
doubting, yet ultimately innocent, Christian.) Despite these gender dif-
ferences, however, the bodies of both Leonor and Antônio are placed on
display for the torturers as well as the spectator of the film: the viewer,
in this sense, plays an uncannily similar role to the Inquisitors by occupying the privileged position of "viewer." Like it or not, the spectator
objectifies the tortured body through his unwitting gaze. In the concluding scene of the film, the gaze of the Inquisition officials is then reflected

in the eyes of the crowd during the public burning of alleged heretics. Here, too, the abject, moribund body of the New Christian appears exposed before the greedy onlookers, who shout anti-Semitic epithets typical of the crowds that witnessed historical autos-da-fé. At the same time, the camera is positioned such that the mob also becomes the object of a gaze: here, the gaze of the viewer of the film.

In this sense, then, there exists another aspect to the visibility of torture in Azulay's film that complicates the traditional hierarchy of subject and object, spectator and victim. The interrogation scenes, too, exhibit a kind of ocular complexity that disrupts the notion of the gaze as necessarily violent. Amidst the brutality of the torture, the camera briefly pauses upon the face of the prisoner, exposing, if only for an instant, what Emmanuel Levinas calls the face of the Other, that aspect of the other that demands ethical responsibility in the subject through the figurative enunciation of the command, "Thou shalt not kill." The constitution of ethical subjectivity, for Levinas, lies in the subject's response to the "disclosing of a face," which he describes as "nudity, non-form, abandon of self, ageing, dying, more naked than nudity. It is poverty, skin with wrinkles, which are a trace of itself" (Levinas, *Otherwise than Being*, 88). This momentary glimpse is not shared by the torturer, but rather is reserved for the viewer of the film, who then becomes responsible, a witness to the violence, through this brief but powerful interpellation.[15]

What is unique about this dynamic in Azulay's film is that it is the *visual* that serves as both the condition of possibility and impossibility of the ethical. This of course goes against the very notion of ethics described by Levinas, particularly in his earlier work such as "Reality and Its Shadow," in which he excludes visual representation from the realm of the ethical. Jean-François Lyotard explains Levinas's rejection of the visual as grounded in a Jewish conception of the divine: "In Hebraic ethics representation is forbidden, the eye closes, the ear opens in order to hear the father's word" (quoted in Jay, *Downcast Eyes*, 574). Yet Levinas's later work introduces a challenge to this argument through the idea of the "listening eye" as that which receives and responds to the demand of the Other (Levinas, *Otherwise than Being*, 30, 37, 38). It is through this synesthetic trope that we can begin to understand the double bind of the visual in Azulay's film: the visual allows for the sexualization and objectification of the tortured body while simultaneously demanding a response, or responsibility, in the viewer of the film by making her a witness to the brutality. The fine line between ethics and violence is already announced by Levinas, who explains that "the thematization of a face undoes the face and undoes the approach" (Levinas, *Otherwise than Being*, 94).

The aporetic quality of the encounter with the face, the near-inextricability of ethical responsibility and thematization or violence, is intimately connected to the logic of the specter. A reader of Levinas, Derrida's writing on hauntology seems particularly inflected by the Jewish-Lithuanian philosopher's preoccupation with the question of justice. Derrida's specter, as we have seen in chapter 1, exhibits a corporeal paradox:

> The specter is a paradoxical incorporation, the becoming-body, a certain phenomenal and carnal form of the spirit ... some "thing" that remains difficult to name: neither soul nor body, and both one and the other. For it is flesh and phenomenality that give to the spirit its spectral apparition, but which disappear right away in the apparition, in the very coming of the revenant or the return of the specter. (Derrida, *Specters of Marx*, 5)

If the physicality of the torture victim provokes objectification in the cinematic gaze, this very carnality is accompanied by a stubborn ghost. Visual exposure thus simultaneously allows for the thematization of the body of the other while creating a possible opening for the ethico-political demand. Considered in this light, the radically corporeal scene of torture does not—cannot—stand alone, but rather is always already in relation to the question of the secret, the "secret of *everything*" that haunts each act of torture, demanding justice.

Although we can argue that both Magalhães and Ripstein reproduce Inquisitional logic by preserving the bond between torture and truth, Berman and Azulay take an initial step toward deconstructing interrogation through an emphasis on the performative (Berman) and by forging a link between spectacle and spectrality (Azulay). While Magalhães's play dramatizes contradictory scenes of confession, in which an innocent New Christian professes guilt and a contrite priest absolves himself, but which in both cases serve to cement the church's role in preserving truth through the institution of confession, in Ripstein the torture of Luis successfully produces the names of Judaizers (the "truth") who will all burn at the stake. In both instances, any potential resistance to Inquisitional logic lies in the act of interpretation: the exposure of the link between guilt, desire, and confession in the former, and the reading of the Marxist subtext (and its limits) in the latter. Berman and Azulay, on the other hand, sow the discursive seeds for a possible relationship between aesthetics, ethics, and politics in their interpellation of the viewer, even when such interpellation is intimately bound to the subjection of the protagonists. If Berman—by constructing a Kafkaesque closed system while simultaneously bringing to the fore the limit of such a system—signals the possibility of refused identification, Azulay's spectral torture victims demand justice by disrupting the traditional economy of the gaze. In the following chapter I ask whether it is possible, through figurative language, to disentangle fully the relationship between torture and truth that lies at the heart of interrogation as well as its aesthetic representation. Can the spectral quality of the interrogated subject puncture a hole in Inquisitional logic? What would it mean for a work of art to deconstruct the act of questioning? Would it mean that such a work of art forecloses all the possible modes in which the act of questioning could be recovered? What, finally, is the relation between what we could call the deconstructive drive of certain works of art, on one hand, and on the other Inquisitional logic, the logic of the question concerning identity?

CHAPTER 4

Other Inquisitions

In the introduction to this book, I refer to the way in which Gilles Pontecorvo's provocative film *The Battle of Algiers,* which documents through fiction the French torture of Algerians, poses a particularly difficult challenge for thinking the ethicity of the aesthetic representation of torture. Despite the oppositional stance *The Battle of Algiers* takes against the use of torture by the French military, I argue that Pontecorvo does little to dismantle the relationship between torture and truth and that, from the very first scene of the film, the violent interrogation of prisoners is shown to extract the "truth" (specifically, the names of FLN operatives) from the body of the other. That one of the earliest cinematic protests against the use of torture ends up reproducing the very logic that makes torture possible points to a highly complex—and problematic— relationship between ethics, politics, and aesthetics in the representation of interrogation.

In many of the Inquisition narratives I have discussed in the previous three chapters, there exists a tension between the reproduction of Inquisitional logic, on the one hand, and the deconstruction of such logic. The relationship between torture and truth detailed by Page duBois—in which the violent interrogation of the Athenian slave is thought to extract the truth in each and every case—anticipates the logic of the Inquisition, according to which the marrano is either a faithful Christian or a "secret" Judaizer. This logic is often echoed in the cinematographic and dramatic works that represent this historical period, even when these

works seek to voice resistance to the violent persecution of the marrano (and the contemporary violent acts that these allegorical scenes
imply). If an aesthetic critique of torture can paradoxically preserve the
very logic that makes its existence possible, how might we imagine a
literary approach to torture that would move beyond a mere moral or
ideological stance against the practice? How might literary language
subvert or insubordinate (legal, political, moral) discourses that reproduce totalitarian or totalizing thinking even as they strive to condemn
it? In what way can we begin to think about a logic of truth—an ethic
of truth—that could destabilize the practice of torture and Inquisitional
logic more broadly?

SEEING AND SAYING: SARAMAGO'S *LUCIDEZ*

How to prove by bearing witness, if testimony remains
irreducibly heterogeneous to proof?
—Jacques Derrida

. . . now just imagine if I had asked if you wanted to
go to bed with me, what would you have said then,
what would the machine have said . . .
—José Saramago

In order to address these preoccupations, I would like to take a step
back from the corpus of Inquisition narratives that have comprised the
main corpus of this study, and turn to José Saramago's 2004 *Ensaio
sobre a Lucidez,* a novel that bears witness to the Inquisitional logic
that dominates dictatorship and post-dictatorship Portugal, as well as
the broader global landscape following the attacks of September 11,
2001.[1] Translated into English as *Seeing,* the novel functions as a sequel
to Saramago's 1995 *Ensaio sobre a Ceguera* (*Blindness*), in which the
citizens of an entire city lose their sight in a mysterious epidemic that
ultimately leads to anarchy. In *Seeing,* the government of the same unnamed country[2] declares a state of emergency (*estado de excepção*) following the casting of over 70 percent blank ballots during a municipal
election, four years after the inhabitants of the city have regained their
sight and democracy has ostensibly been restored. As the government
begins to record the conversations of voters and arrest and interrogate
citizens at random, the novel evolves into an indirect meditation upon

the questionable tactics used in recent years in the so-called war on terror. I will focus my discussion upon three scenes of interrogation in order to consider the possibility of the deconstruction of interrogation through the literary. My argument is that Saramago subverts the "truth" of the lie detector by suggesting that the event of truth (or the truth of the event) disrupts any intent to control information through interrogation (or, for that matter, through any narrative, including the novel itself). Placing Saramago's notion of "seeing" alongside Emmanuel Levinas's idea of "saying" (*le dire*), I want to ask how literature might interrupt or sabotage the act of torture. Is it possible to think, together with Jacques Derrida, the logic of the machine—here, the polygraph—together with the logic of the event? What are the ethical and political implications of the representation of interrogation by the literary?

Written in the wake of September 11, 2001, Saramago's *Seeing* offers a scathing account of contemporary Western politics, exposing the ways in which allegedly democratic governments seek to preserve power. A week following the designated election day (on which no one appears to vote until precisely four o'clock, at which time crowds of people flood the polling places and cast an overwhelming number of blank votes), a second election is called. This time, the government monitors the polling places, recording the conversations of voters with the intention of gathering information that will lead them to the core of what they believe to be an organized conspiracy against the ruling party. The intelligence-gathering is portrayed by the narrator as flawed, as technology and human error come together to yield misreadings of the data:

> As informações choviam na central à medida que o tempo ia passando, porém em nenhum caso revelavam de uma forma clara e portanto futuramente irrebatível a intenção de voto do eleitor caçado, o mais que na lista se encontrava eram frases do tipo das acimas mencionadas, e até aquela que se afigurava mais suspeitosa, Algum dia teria de acontecer, perderia muito da sua aparente periculosidade se a restituíssem ao seu contexto, nada mais que uma conversa de dois homens sobre o recente divórcio de um deles, toda conduzida por meias palavras para não excitar a curiosidade das pessoas próximas, e que daquele modo havia concluído, com um tanto de rancoroso, com um tanto de resignado, mas que o trémulo suspiro saído do peito do homem que se divorciara, fosse a sensibilidade o melhor atributo do ofício de

espia, deveria ter feito pender claramente para o quadrante
da resignação. Que o espia não o tivesse considerado digno
de nota, que o gravador não o tivesse captado, são falhas hu-
manas e desacertos tecnológicos cuja simples eventualidade
o bom juiz, sabendo o que são os homens e não ignorando
o que são as máquinas, teria o dever de tomar em conta,
mesmo que, e isso sim seria magnificamente justo, ainda que
à primeira vista pudesse parecer escandaloso, não houvesse
na matéria do processo o mais pequeno indício de não culpa-
bilidade do acusado. Trememos só de pensar no que amanhã
poderá suceder àquele inocente se o levam a interrogatório
. . . (Saramago, *Ensaio sobre a Lucidez*, 33)

As the hours passed, information rained down upon the center of operations, but none of it revealed in a clear-cut and
consequently irrefutable manner the intentions of the voter
thus caught, all that appeared on the list were phrases of the
kind described above, and even the phrase that seemed more
suspicious than all the others, well, I suppose it was bound
to happen some time, would lose much of its apparent slip-
periness once restored to its context, a conversation between
two men about the recent divorce of one of them, not that
they spoke of it explicitly, in order not to arouse the curiosity
of the people nearby, but which had concluded thus, with a
touch of rancor, a touch of resignation, and with a tremulous
sigh that came forth from the divorced man's breast and that
should have led any sensitive spy, assuming, of course, that
sensitivity is a spy's best attribute, to come down clearly on
the side of resignation. The fact that the spy may not have
considered this worthy of note, and that the recording equip-
ment may not have captured it, can be put down to mere human failure and to technological blips which any good judge,
knowing what men are like, and not unaware either of the
nature of machines, would have to take into account, even
if, and, although at first sight this may appear shocking, it
would, in fact, be magnificently just, even if in the documents
bearing on the case there was not the slightest indication of
the accused's non-culpability. Were this innocent man to be
interrogated tomorrow, we tremble at the mere thought of
what could happen to him . . . (Saramago, *Seeing*, 23)

Beyond merely highlighting the way in which an innocent man can be mistakenly accused of guilt, this rich passage directly tackles the problem of language and meaning inherent to "intelligence-gathering." To begin with, the quantity of information seems indirectly proportional to the quality of intelligence: despite the fact that "information rained down upon the center of operations," the spies appear unable to decipher correctly the clues that come pouring in. Distancing itself from the assumption that information can successfully be transmitted from person to person, citizen to investigator, voice to machine, interrogated to interrogator, Saramago's narrator reveals the process by which words are taken out of context and imbued with meaning according to ideological necessity. "I suppose it was bound to happen some time" ceases to refer to the divorce of the unfortunate speaker, whose sigh goes unperceived by the spy assigned to the polling place, and instead is interpreted as a subversive statement linked to the electoral crisis. The narrator does not merely announce an injustice here, but rather deconstructs the entire process of intelligence-gathering: what is missing in the erroneous interpretation is not only the context of the original conversation, but the feeling of resignation in the divorcé's sigh. The idea that affect or emotion—and its relationship to the *machinal*—is central to sense-making will become a crucial element of Saramago's treatment of "truth" as the plot develops.

The narrator alludes to the potentially violent consequences of the spy's incompetence in the last sentence, "Were this innocent man to be interrogated tomorrow, we tremble at the mere thought of what could happen to him . . ." The use of the subjunctive and the conditional (a mode that is repeated throughout the novel) distinguishes the narrative from the bounds of the testimonial genre that plays a significant role in post-dictatorship Latin American literature. It articulates a tentativeness that is more haunting than accusatory, reminiscent of Derrida's mode of the "perhaps" in *Specters of Marx*.[3] Rather than explicitly describing the torture that may be used in his questioning (as does *The Battle of Algiers*), the statement is instead punctuated by an ellipsis that alludes to but does not name directly the potential violation of an innocent man. In this way, the concluding sentence radicalizes the limits of language alluded to earlier in the passage. The chasm between information-gathering and sense-making widens, along with the gap between signifier and signified: truth, it seems, lies elsewhere.

The more the police record and analyze the conversations of voters hoping to identify a guilty party responsible for the voting conspiracy, the more their efforts prove futile. In the following passage, the narrator pairs random pieces of conversation picked up by the recording devices with the ridiculous yet threatening questions posed by the police:

> Frases simples, correntes, como as que se seguem, Em geral não costumo votar, mas hoje deu-me para aqui, A ver se isto vai servir para alguma coisa que valha a pena, Tantas vezes foi o cântaro à fonte, que por fim lá deixou ficar a asa, No outro dia também votei, mas só pude sair de casa às quatro, Isto é como a lotaria, quase sempre sai branco, Ainda assim, há que persistir, A esperança é como o sal, não alimenta, mas dá sabor ao pão, durante horas e horas estas e mil outras frases igualmente neutras, igualmente inocentes de culpa, foram esmiuçadas até à última sílaba, esfareladas, viradas do avesso, pisadas no almofariz sob o pilão das perguntas, Explique-me que cântaro é esse, Porque é que a asa se soltou na fonte, e não durante o caminho, ou em casa, Se não era seu costume votar, porque é que votou desta vez, Se a esperança é como o sal, que acha que deveria ser feito para que o sal fosse como a esperança, Como resolveria a diferença de cores entre a esperança, que é verde, e o sal, que é branco, Acha realmente que o boletim de voto é igual a um bilhete de lotaria, Que era o que estava a querer dizer quando disse a palavra branco. (Saramago, *Ensaio sobre a Lucidez*, 48–49)

> Simple, ordinary expressions, such as, I don't generally bother to vote, but here I am, Do you think it'll turn out to have been worth all the bother, The pitcher goes so often to the well that, in the end, it leaves its handle there, I voted last week too, but that day I could only leave home at four, This is just like the lottery, I almost always draw a blank, Still, you've got to keep trying, Hope is like salt, there's no nourishment in it, but it gives the bread its savor, for hours and hours, these and a thousand other equally innocuous, equally neutral, equally innocent phrases were picked apart syllable by syllable, reduced to mere crumbs, turned upside down, crushed in the mortar by the pestle of the question, Explain to me again that business about the pitcher, Why did the handle come off at the well and not on the way there or back, If you don't normally vote, why did you vote this

time, If hope is like salt, what do you think should be done to make salt like hope, How would you resolve the difference in color between hope, which is green, and salt, which is white, Do you really think that a ballot paper is the same as a lottery ticket, What did you mean when you used the word blank. (Saramago, *Seeing*, 38)

The above citation, taken from an even longer sentence that fills a page and a half of the novel, begins with a slew of examples of arbitrary, insignificant phrases collected by the recording devices, and ends with an equally absurd series of questions meant to decipher the voters' petty banter, but which instead signal a void at the heart of the investigation (signaled metonymically by the "blank" vote). Saramago cleverly juxtaposes the figurative speech of the tapped subjects with the literal questions of the interrogators who, in their inability to comprehend the abstract, cannot possibly decode the meaning of the phrases. In addition to indicating a discursive violence in the act of questioning through the motif of the mortar and pestle (the question "crushes" the answer), the creative process inherent in the act of interrogation is also insinuated in this passage, in which paranoia and imagination come together to generate in an automatic, repetitive, machine-like way, the guilty subject. The guilty subject, for its part, is represented as constructed by making the process of fabricating guilt transparent through parody.

The first scene of interrogation I'd like to discuss concerns an innocent woman whom the police question using a lie detector test. This scene, in which the unhappy marriage of language and technology produces a flawed method of information gathering, reveals a series of hidden, unaccounted-for factors in the art of questioning. The interrogation is introduced by the narrator with a description of how the polygraph functions:

> Ligado à máquina por um emaranhado de cabos, braçadeiras e ventosas, o paciente não sofre, só tem de dizer a verdade, toda a verdade e só a verdade, e, já agora, não crer, ele próprio, na asserção universal que desde o princípio dos tempos nos anda a atroar os ouvidos com a balela de que a vontade tudo pode, aqui está, para não irmos mais longe, um exemplo que flagrantemente o nega, pois essa tua estupenda vontade, por muito que te fies nela, por mais tenaz que se tenha mostrado até hoje, não poderá controlar as crispações

dos teus músculos, estancar a sudação inconveniente, impedir a palpitação das pálpebras, disciplinar a respiração. No fim dir-te-ão que mentiste, tu negarás, jurarás que disseste a verdade, toda a verdade e só a verdade, e talvez seja certo, não mentiste, o que acontece é que és uma pessoa nervosa, de vontade forte, sim, mas como uma espécie de trémulo junco que a mínima aragem faz estremecer, tornarão a atarte à máquina e então será muito pior, perguntar-te-ão se estás vivo e tu, claro está, responderás que sim, mas o teu corpo protestará, desmentir-te-á, o tremor do teu queixo dirá que não, que estás morto, e se calhar tem razão, talvez, antes de ti, o teu corpo saiba já que te vão matar. (Saramago, *Ensaio sobre a Lucidez,* 55–56)

Connected to the machine by a tangle of wires, armbands and suction pads, the patient does not suffer, he simply has to tell the truth, the whole truth and nothing but the truth, and to cease to believe in the universal assertion, the old, old story, which, since the beginning of time, has been drummed into us, that the will can do anything, for you need look no further than the following example, which denies it outright, because that wonderful will of yours, however much you may trust it, however tenacious it may have been up until now, cannot control twitching muscles, cannot staunch unwanted sweat or stop eyelids blinking or regulate breathing. In the end, they'll say you lied, you'll deny it, you'll swear you told the truth, the whole truth and nothing but the truth, and that might be true, you didn't lie, you just happen to be a very nervous person, with a strong will, it's true, but you are nevertheless a tremulous reed that shivers in the slightest breeze, so they'll connect you up to the machine again and it will be even worse, they'll ask you if you're alive and you'll say, of course I am, but your body will protest, will contradict you, the tremor in your chin will say no, you're dead, and it might be right, perhaps your body knows before you do that they are going to kill you. (Saramago, *Seeing,* 45)

The polygraph, like the medieval torture device, is imbued with the power to extract truth. The ostensibly nonviolent, "modern" version of the torture device relies, perhaps counterintuitively, upon an aspect of the self that defies what is a distinctly modern conception of subjectivity: the notion that the subject is rooted in a unified, autonomous will.[4] Saramago's narrator explains that the polygraph is thought to "work" by exposing an aspect of the subject that remains hidden: the involuntary reflex (the "other side" of the prisoner's confession) betrays the coherent discourse pronounced by the interrogated subject. Any attempt to lie (or even to tell the truth) can be sabotaged by the subject's own body: a twitch, a blink, a tremor, perspiration, even one's own breath. The motif of the involuntary reflex indicates an entire field of experience that can completely incapacitate the autonomous will.

The fact that one can claim to be alive while the body, through the involuntary reflex, reveals one to be dead is a particularly poignant example of Saramago's subversion of the logic of truth, or the logic of the truth of interrogation. In this extreme instance, the lie detector actually proves effectual, while simultaneously calling into question our very notion of what it means to tell the truth. The machine can "accurately" perceive the lie (the prisoner claims to be alive when she is, in fact, dead), even as this truth appears to be disproved by the prisoner's (living) body. Saramago seems less interested in whether the lie detector is accurate or inaccurate, and more concerned with a question of truth that goes beyond empirical information: the body, alive in an observable sense, knows on some level that it will soon be killed, revealing the "Truth" of the situation, that is, the violence that is the truth of interrogation. This hypothetical scenario is qualified by the word "perhaps," suggestive of a kind of Derridean undecidability that, I will argue, is central to Saramago's interpretation of the relationship between truth and lie. The use of the verb "desmentir" to indicate the kind of truth that might escape the prisoner's body against the will of the prisoner is highly evocative: the idea of "unlying" alludes to the possibility of a truth that is more deconstructive than fixed, a saying rather than a said.

The relationship of undecidability between truth and lie or, more precisely, between truth-telling and lying, is treated by Derrida in his analysis of the confession in "Typewriter Ribbon."[5] If in "History of the Lie" the philosopher distinguishes between lying as an intentional act and the "lie"—"there is not the lie, but rather this saying or this meaning-to-say that is called lying" (34)—the act of confession or telling the truth (the Levinasian "saying") must be understood as distinct from the truth (the "said"). Simon Critchley explains that in Levinas "the saying . . . is the performative stating, proposing or expressive position of myself facing the other. It is a verbal and possibly also non-verbal ethical performance, of which the essence cannot be captured in constative propositions . . . [while] the said is a statement, assertion or proposition of which the truth or falsity can be ascertained" (18). In "Typewriter Ribbon," Derrida turns to Paul de Man's reading of Jean-Jacques Rousseau's *Confessions*, in particular, Rousseau's admission of the theft of a "pink and silver colored ribbon" while working for an aristocratic family in Turin (to which I refer in the previous chapter). Without entering into a detailed discussion of Rousseau's youthful transgression and subsequent profession of guilt, I would like to focus upon a central aspect of Derrida's analysis of the place of truth in the act of confession. While de Man argues for a consideration of the performative rather than the cognitive or constative dimension of confession, Derrida insists upon a simultaneous consideration of both through the mutual analysis of the logic of the event and the logic of the machine. Rather than positing the repetition of the machine against the singularity of the event, he highlights the inseparability of the constative and performative dimensions of confession through the Greek notion of *mēkhanē*, "at once an ingenious theatrical machine or a war machine, thus a machine and a machination, something both mechanical and strategic" (Derrida, "Typewriter Ribbon," 71).

In the scene in question in Saramago, one can point to the constative aspect of the confession (e.g., *I cast a blank vote, I did not cast a blank vote, I am alive*) together with the performative dimension of the involuntary reflex (*I am going to die*), which exceeds or discredits the constative or cognitive. In the constative understanding of confession, the prisoner, under torture or threat of torture, tells the truth. Or even: the prisoner, under torture or threat of torture, intentionally lies in order to stop the torture. In either scenario, the emphasis remains on the content of the confession, the said, rather than the saying. We are correct in underscoring (as does de Man) the performative aspect of confessional discourse, the truth of the event as that which *happens* or comes into existence through the act of confessing. But it is also useful to consider the mutual contamination of machine and event. Indeed, Levinas reveals the inseparability of the saying and the said: "The correlation of the saying and the said, that is, the subordination of the saying to the said, to the linguistic system and to ontology, is the price that manifestation demands. In language qua said everything is conveyed before us, be it at the price of a betrayal" (Levinas, *Otherwise than Being*, 6). For Saramago, the machine (here, the polygraph) is an imperfect device. Like the tape recorder that fails to gather "accurate" intelligence in the earlier scene, the polygraph reads the truth of the body but misinterprets it: the machine fails to read or misreads the body of the other. Yet to reduce the discourse of interrogation to that which hails from the polygraph as machine is to overlook the difference that is created through the act of interrogation. Where is it located, where is it produced? It is here that the act of interpretation once again becomes decisive:

> Um polígrafo, íamos dizendo, não consegue ir a parte nenhuma sem ajuda, necessita ter ao seu lado um técnico habilitado que lhe interprete os riscos traçados no papel, mas isto não quer dizer que o dito técnico seja conhecedor da verdade, o que ele sabe é só aquilo que está diante dos seus olhos, que a pergunta feita ao paciente sob observação produziu o que poderíamos chamar, inovadoramente, uma reacção alergográfica, ou, em palavras mais literárias mas não menos imaginativas, o desenho da mentira. (Saramago, *Ensaio sobre a Lucidez,* 57)

> A polygraph, as we were saying, cannot go anywhere without help, it needs to have by its side a trained technician who can interpret the lines on the paper, but this doesn't mean that the technician must be a connoisseur of the truth, all he has to know is what is there before his eyes, that the question asked of the patient under observation has produced what we might innovatively call an allergographic reaction, or in more literary but no less imaginative terms, the outline of a lie. (Saramago, *Seeing,* 46)

The technician is therefore characterized as a reader of sorts, a reader of the text generated by the lie detector machine, "uma folha de papel húmido impregnado de iodeto de potássio e amido" (Saramago, *Ensaio sobre a Lucidez,* 55) ("a sheet of damp paper impregnated with potassium iodide and starch") (Saramago, *Seeing,* 45). Distinct, to be sure, from the "writing machine" detailed by Derrida in "Typewritter Ribbon," the polygraph nonetheless engenders a text that demands decodification, even when this demand fails to be fulfilled (either because it is misinterpreted, or because it is fundamentally uninterpretable).

The scene reflects further upon the precarious art of interpretation and the truth of the lie detector as a suspect arrives to be questioned by a young, inexperienced secret service agent. That the suspect is depicted as "certa mulher, nova e bonita [. . . uma] mata-hari" (Saramago, *Ensaio sobre a Lucidez*, 58) ("a pretty young woman [. . . a] mata-hari") (Saramago, *Seeing*, 47) brings to the discussion the question of desire, to which I will return below. After the polygraph finds the young woman guilty (the first of two women who will represent the voice of "truth" in the novel), the "mata-hari" proceeds to challenge the validity of the machine by arguing for a consideration of emotion: "Não somos robôs nem pedras falantes, senhor agente, disse a mulher, em toda a verdade humana há sempre algo de angustioso, de aflito . . . somos uma pequena e trémula chama que a cada instante ameaça apagar-se, e temos medo" (58) ("We're not robots or talking stones, mister agent, said the woman, and within every human truth there is always an element of anxiety or conflict . . . we are a small, tremulous flame which threatens at any moment to go out, and we are afraid" (48). Placing the machine ("we're not robots") in opposition to affect ("we are afraid"), the interrogated woman then proposes that they reverse roles, that she act as the interrogator and he the interrogated, in order to illustrate her point. Attached to the polygraph, sure enough, the agent's declaration of innocence shows up as a lie on the "damp paper." The woman reassures the shaken agent, "acredito que tenha dito a verdade, que não votou em branco nem votará, mas recordo-lhe que não era disso que se tratava, eu só pretendi demonstrar-lhe, e consegui, que não nos podemos fiar demasiado no nosso corpo" (59) ("I believe you told the truth, that you didn't cast a blank vote and never will, but that, I must remind you, is not the point, I was just trying to demonstrate to you, successfully as it turns out, that we cannot entirely trust our bodies") (49). The narrator therefore distinguishes between "truth," which "is not the point," and "Truth," which proves more elusive. Recalling the earlier account of the body's response to the polygraph ("perhaps your body knows before you do") complicates the woman's assertion that the agent is innocent. While he may be innocent of having cast a blank vote, we could in theory understand him as guilty in a broader sense: guilty of interrogating an innocent woman, guilty of desiring her. His body knows more than his will. The woman acknowledges the ambivalent quality of confession by declaring that "as astúcias não serviram de nada, que nós todos continuaremos a mentir quando dissermos a verdade, que continuaremos a dizer a verdade quando estivermos a mentir . . . agora imagine que eu lhe tinha perguntado se queria ir a cama comigo, que responderia, que diria a máquina" (60) ("no amount of cunning will do any good, we will all continue to lie when we tell the truth, and to tell the truth when we lie . . . now just imagine if I had asked if you wanted to go to bed with me, what would you have said then, what would the machine have said") (49). Her final statement, which echoes the subjunctive mode discussed earlier, makes several observations worth commenting upon: (1) it proposes a reading of truth-telling as lying and lying as truth-telling, (2) it reveals a relationship between desire, guilt, and truth, and (3) it underscores the automaticity of confession through the idea of the talking machine.

The notion of automatic speech finds a curious echo in de Man's and Derrida's readings of Rousseau's curiously worded attribution of the theft to Marion, another servant in the Turin household, when questioned: "It is certain that neither my judgment, nor my will dictated my reply, but that it was the automatic result [*l'effet machinal*] of my embarrassment" (qtd. in Derrida, "Typewriter Ribbon," 156). It is here that we begin to understand that affect and machine do not exist in opposition but rather in intimate relation to one another. Rousseau's embarrassment does not appear as a force counter to the machine, but *machinal*, automatic in itself. Embarrassment (or guilt, or desire) counterintuitively operates as machine, upending the will, *even as it exceeds the logic of the machine*. Finally, desire understood as exposure or opening to the other can be read as vital to the "Truth" of interrogation: it is ultimately the agent's desire for the attractive prisoner that heralds his downfall.

I would now like to turn to two final scenes of questioning that take place close to the end of the novel, at which time a police superintendent has been sent back into the capital city (which the politicians, military, and police have abandoned, fearing a violent uprising) in order to pursue a lead that the authorities received in a letter addressed to the prime minister. The return of the superintendent to the city marks a shift in the plot, which until this point has been narrated from a distance, without focusing upon any character in particular. Through the investigation of the letter, a protagonist is born, who (I will argue) is constituted as an ethical subject through his response to the *eventness* of interrogation. The letter the superintendent and his two assistants are investigating (under order of the prime minister himself) refers back to the period of blindness four years earlier, in which the citizens of the capital city found themselves struck by an epidemic of blindness, the city disintegrated into anarchy, and an untold number of people died of natural and unnatural causes alike. The contents of the letter reveal that one woman mysteriously—miraculously—did not lose her sight like the others, and implies that this exceptionality is cause for suspicion. According to the then-blind witness, the woman—the wife of an ophthalmologist—committed a murder during the period of the epidemic.

When the police visit the author of the defamatory letter in order to question him, they learn that the murder was committed in defense of a group of women who were being raped by a gang of men in exchange for food for the women's male companions. The officers discover, through interrogation, that the author of the letter was among those who in effect bought food with their wives' bodies and that, following the end of the epidemic, he divorced his wife as a result.

> Vê algum inconveniente em dizer-nos por que se divorciaram, Motivos pessoais, Claro que teriam de ser pessoais, Motivos íntimos, Como em todos os divórcios. O homem olhou os insondáveis rostos que tinha na sua frente e compreendeu que não o deixariam em sossego enquanto não lhes dissesse o que queriam. . . . Teve tudo que ver com os tais cegos, não pude suportar que a minha mulher se tivesse ido meter debaixo daqueles bandidos, durante um ano ainda aguentei a vergonha, mas por fim tornou-se-me insuportável, separei-me, divorcei-me, Uma curiosidade, creio ter-lhe ouvido que os outros cegos cediam a comida em paga das mulheres, disse o inspector, Assim era, Suponho, portanto, que os seus princípios não lhe permitiram tocar no alimento que a sua mulher lhe trouxe depois de se ter ido meter debaixo daqueles bandidos, para usar a sua enérgica expressão. O homem baixou a cabeça e não respondeu. (Saramago, *Ensaio sobre a Lucidez*, 217)

> Would you object to telling us why you got divorced, For personal reasons, Naturally they would be personal, For private reasons then, As with all divorces. The man looked at the inscrutable faces before him and realized that they would not leave him in peace until he had told them what they wanted to know. . . . It was to do with those blind men, I couldn't bear the fact that my wife had done it with those vile men, for a whole year I put up with the shame of it, but, in the end, it became unbearable, and so I left her, got a divorce, How odd, I thought you said that these other blind men gave you food in exchange for your women, said the inspector, That's right, And your principles, I assume, did not

allow you to touch the food that your wife brought to you after she had, to use your expression, done it with those vile men. The man hung his head and did not reply. (Saramago, *Seeing*, 199)

In a matter of several sentences, the dialogue between police and (innocent) witness evolves into an exchange between police and (guilty) subject. By echoing, subtly manipulating and thus reversing the meaning of the witness's words (personal, private, done it, vile men, principles), the interrogator (who does not need recourse to a polygraph nor violence, threatened or real) teases out the truth of the matter, which has nothing to do with the electoral enigma. The divorced man, the interrogation reveals, is guilty of the most heinous of crimes: offering his wife's body to rapists in exchange for food, later abandoning his wife for what is in reality is *his* crime. Saramago's distinctive narrative style, which bears more resemblance to oral speech than to normative grammatical writing, and in which punctuation beyond commas and periods is virtually nonexistent, creates a curious form of interrogation. Here, questions and answers appear indistinguishable, or at the very least interchangeable: the phrases of the interrogated can thus be appropriated quite easily by the interrogator. In addition to exposing the way in which the malleability of language contributes to the construction of meaning in the interrogation, this scene demonstrates the way in which it is the accuser, rather than the accused, who stands as the guilty subject within the broader context of the election crisis. The narrator communicates the man's guilt not through explicit confession, according to a logic of the legal, but through a different logic, that of the literary: nuance, manipulation of meaning and, finally, silence.

The superintendent then pays a visit to the ophthalmologist's wife, who not only appears innocent of having had anything to do with the unexplained blank votes but, on the contrary, proves to be the epitome of innocence and heroism. Arriving at her house with the sole intention of gathering information about the blank votes, his queries are met with a series of biting questions of her own.

Polícia, disse, E que pretende a polícia das pessoas que vivem nesta casa, perguntou a mulher, Que respondam a algumas perguntas, Sobre que assunto, Não creio que um patamar de escada seja o lugar mais próprio para dar princípio a um interrogatório, Trata-se então de um interrogatório, perguntou a mulher, Minha senhora, ainda que eu só tivesse duas perguntas para lhe fazer, isso já seria um interrogatório, Vejo que aprecia a precisão de linguagem, Sobretudo nas respostas que me dão, Essa, sim, que é uma boa resposta, Não era difícil, serviu-me de bandeja, Servir-lhe-ei outras, se vem à procura de alguma verdade, Procurar a verdade é o objectivo fundmaental de qualquer polícia. (Saramago, *Ensaio sobre a Lucidez*, 230)

Police, he said, And what do the police want with the people who live in this apartment, asked the woman, The answers to a few questions, About what, Look, I hardly think the landing is the best place to begin an interrogation, Oh, so it's an interrogation, is it, asked the woman, Madam, even if I only had two questions to ask you, it would still be an interrogation, You appreciate precision in language I see, Especially in the answers I am given, Now that's a good answer, It wasn't difficult, you served it up to me on a plate, And I'll serve you up some others if what you're after is the truth, Looking for the truth is the fundamental aim of any policeman. (Saramago, *Seeing*, 210–11)

The responses given to the superintendent predominantly take the form of sarcastic yet clever probes (what do the police want, about what, so it's an interrogation), indicating not only that the superintendent has met his match (or superior) in terms of intelligence, but that the interrogated subject here may be the bearer of a truth: not the truth of facts, but that of the event in a Badiouian sense. It is her demand that truth take precedence in the case that will ultimately determine the outcome of her interrogation.

In the end, it is not the wit of the ophthalmologist's wife that overcomes the officer, but rather the image of her that is revealed to him as a nurturer of the group of blind citizens that rattles him: he is literally thrown off course by the idea that he, too, might have had someone to care for him during that dark period, someone who, for one, might have saved the lives of his parents. This realization comes to him by way of a final confrontation with the ophthalmologist's wife, this one hypothetical. In this imagined scenario, the superintendent starts out strong, authoritative voice intact, with the intention to question but succumbs, finally, to affect.

Que interrogatório, pensou, dizer-lhe, por exemplo, a senhora é suspeita de ser a organizadora, a responsável, a dirigente máxima do movimento subversivo que veio pôr em grave perigo o sistema democrático ... uma vez que as provas tenha a senhora a certeza de que hão-de aparecer quando forem precisas, é só questão de inventar uma ou duas que sejam irrefutáveis, e ainda que não o pudessem ser completamente, as provas circunstanciais, mesmo que remotas, nos bastariam, como o facto incompreensível de a senhora não ter cegado há quatro anos ... é esta, ainda que expressada noutros termos, a opinião do meu ministro, que eu tenho obrigação de acatar mesmo que me doa a coração ... se lhe falo assim é porque a senhora me cai bem, e para que veja até que ponto vai a minha simpatia, só lhe direi que a maior felicidade da minha vida, há quatro anos, tirando não ter perdido parte da família naquela tragédia, como desgraçadamente perdi, teria sido andar junto com o grupo que a senhora protegeu ... se tudo isso e muito mais tivesse acontecido eu poderia declarar sob palavra de honra ao ministro do interior que ele está enganado, que uma experiência como aquela e quatro anos de amizado dão para conhecer bem uma pessoa, e afinal, veja lá, entrei em sua casa como um inimigo e agora não sei como sair dela. (Saramago, *Ensaio sobre a Lucidez,* 251–53)

What interrogation, he thought, would he say to her, for example, you are suspected of being the organizer, the leader, the king-pin of the subversive movement that has placed democracy in such grave danger ... you can be quite sure, madam, that the proof will appear when it's needed, it's just a matter of inventing one or two irrefutable ones, and even if they're not completely irrefutable, the circumstantial evidence, however remote in time, will be enough for us, as will the incomprehensible fact that you did not go blind four years ago ... that, at least, albeit expressed in different words, is the opinion of my minister, whom I have to obey even if it makes my heart ache ... the reason I'm speaking to you in this way is because I like you, and just so that you can see how much I like you, I will tell you that the greatest happiness life could have given me four years ago, apart from

not having lost part of my family in that tragedy, which, alas,
I did, would have been to be a member of the group that you
protected . . . if all that and more had happened, I would be
able to declare on my word of honor to the interior minister
that he is wrong, that an experience like that and four years
of friendship are enough for anyone to say that they know a
person well, and think that I entered your house as an enemy
and now don't know how to leave it. (Saramago, *Seeing*,
232–33)

The meeting with the ophthalmologist's wife therefore precipitates a
radical shift in the inspector, who is transformed, in a matter of pages,
from obedient interrogator to a subject that is faithful to an event of
truth. After encountering the undeniability of the Real in the figure of
the woman who did not succumb to blindness four years before—and
who, now, rejects the entire apparatus of power that would seek to
accuse her (or anyone) of conspiracy—the inspector finds himself interrupted, suspended. Having been struck by this event of truth, he now
has no choice but to remain faithful to that which has broken him.

I believe this is what Alain Badiou describes in *Ethics: An Essay on
the Understanding of Evil*, in which he outlines a theory of ethics as
fidelity to a truth-process. Inspired by the Lacanian dictum to not give
way on one's desire (*"ne pas céder sur son désir"*), Badiou phrases his
own version of an ethical imperative as "do not give up on your own
seizure by a truth-process" (*Ethics*, 47). For Badiou, then, the ethical
subject would be he who, having been seized by a truth-process, must
act according to this truth: "I call 'subject' the bearer [*le support*] of a
fidelity, the one who bears a process of truth. The subject, therefore, in
no way pre-exists the process. He is absolutely nonexistent in the situation 'before' the event. We might say that the process of truth *induces* a
subject" (43). The superintendent, or the version of the superintendent
that is constituted through the event (or, more precisely, through his
response to the event), decides that he must expose the truth of the situation: he calls the newspaper, confesses, and is murdered the following
day by his superiors.

What does the literary have to tell us about the relationship between
torture and truth? In what way can literary discourse make a unique
contribution to this debate, and what are the limits of such a discourse?
Can the literary disrupt Inquisitional logic by underscoring these limits?

Unlike *The Battle of Algiers* (and nearly all of the Inquisition narratives discussed in this book), Saramago's *Seeing* does not include scenes of torture but merely alludes to the hypothetical possibility of its existence. In addition to the act of torture, the question of the disappeared prisoners is also excluded from the novel. We have already been told by the narrator that 500 people have been arrested at random to be questioned, and that the divorcé, whose sigh is misconstrued as guilt rather than resignation, could suffer indescribably if he were to be included in their numbers: "Were this innocent man to be interrogated tomorrow, we tremble at the mere thought of what could happen to him . . ." the narrator laments, trailing off elliptically (Saramago, *Seeing*, 23). The narrative "tremble" and ellipsis imply an unspeakable horror that does not—cannot—find a place within the confines of the text. Following the polygraph scene discussed earlier, the narrator turns to the question of the whereabouts of the missing voters:

> O que sucedeu àquelas quinhentas pessoas apanhadas nas filas de votantes pelos espiões do ministério do interior, aquelas que sofreram depois tormentosos interrogatórios e tiveram de padecer a agonia de verem os seus segredos mais íntimos devassados pelo detector de mentiras. . . . Sobre [este] ponto, não temos mais que dúvidas e nenhuma possibilidade de as aclarar. Há quem diga que os quinhentos reclusos continuam, de acordo com o conhecido eufemismo policial, a colaborar com as autoridades com vista ao esclarecimento dos factos, outros afirmam que estão a ser postos em liberdade, embora aos poucos de cada vez para não darem demasiado nas vistas, porém, os mais cépticos admitem a versão de que os levaram a todos para fora da cidade, que se encontram em paradeiro desconhecido e que os interrogatórios, não obstante os nulos resultados até agora obtidos, continuan. Vá lá a saber-se quem terá razão. (Saramago, *Ensaio sobre a Lucidez*, 74)

What happened to the five hundred people plucked from the queues of voters by the ministry of the interior's spies and who subsequently underwent the torment of interrogation and the agony of seeing their most intimate secrets revealed by the lie detector. . . . [On this] point, we have only doubts and no way of resolving them. There are those who say that

the five hundred prisoners are, in accordance with that popular police euphemism, still helping the authorities with their
inquiries in the hope of clarifying the facts, others say that
they are gradually being freed, although only a few at a time
so as not to attract too much attention, however, the more
skeptical observers believe a third version, that they have all
been removed from the city and are now in some unknown
location and that, despite the dearth of results obtained hith-
erto, the interrogations continue. Who knows who is right.
(Saramago, *Seeing*, 62–63)

The narrator's doubts together with the "not known" of the prisoners'
whereabouts signal at once the potential violence experienced by the
prisoners (reminiscent of the use of torture at top secret "black sites"
by the U.S. government, perhaps the most recent instantiation of the
state of exception) as well as the limits of a narrative that would seek to
represent this violence.

Even as Saramago's novel seems to assign a certain redemptive quality to literary discourse, then, it simultaneously signals the limits of such
a discourse:

O inconveniente destas digressões narrativas, ocupados
como estivemos com intrometidos excursos, é acabar por
descobrir, porém demasiado tarde, que, mal nos tínhamos
precatado, os acontecimentos não esperaram por nós, que já
lá vão adiante, e que em lugar de havermos anunciado, como
é elementar obrigação de qualquer contador de histórias que
saiba do seu ofício, o que iria suceder, não nos resta agora
outro remédio que confessar, contritos, que já sucedeu. (Saramago, *Ensaio sobre a Lucidez*, 139)

The trouble with these narrative digressions, taken up as we
have been with bothersome detours, is that one can find,
too late, of course, almost without noticing, that events have
moved on, have gone on ahead, and instead of us announcing what is about to happen, which is, after all, the elemen-
tary duty of any teller of tales worth his salt, all we can do
is confess contritely that it already has. (Saramago, *Seeing*,
124–25)

The event, once again, triumphs as it races past the meandering narrative that seeks to anticipate or represent it. Just as the involuntary reflex conquers the will of the confessor, just as desire overcomes the machine, just as affect immobilizes the interrogator, the event renders narrative impotent. It is not a coincidence that the narrator announces his own failure using the language of confession ("all we can do is confess"). Faced with the impossible task of truth-telling, the narrative subject turns to the only discourse left within the scene of interrogation: confession, at once an admission of guilt, of fallibility, and a statement of truth that paradoxically reinvests the voice with authority.

How can literary discourse succeed in providing insight into debates on torture and truth where other discourses fall short? What does the literary have to say about interrogation and confession that cannot be addressed by scientific or legal discourses (particularly when it says that it cannot say)? By way of conclusion, I would like to suggest that it is because scientific and legal discourses must obey a logic of proof while literary discourse may obey a logic of testimony. Pontecorvo's *The Battle of Algiers* (as well as Inquisition stories such as Ripstein's *El Santo Oficio,* Magalhães's *O Poeta e a inquisição,* or Santareno's *O Judeu*) seems to remain loyal to the logic of proof, and therefore resides within the realm of the moral rather than the ethical: these works of art tend to moralize rather than expose, communicate a said rather than a saying. In "History of the Lie," Derrida asks how it is possible "to prove by bearing witness, if testimony remains irreducibly heterogeneous to proof" (52). In this sense, *Seeing* (as literature) *necessarily fails to prove* without a doubt that the polygraph works or does not work, elicits accurate information or not. Instead, it deconstructs the entire scene of questioning and confession in order to testify to the void at the core of what is traditionally understood by "truth" and "lie."

Why is it that the textual example that goes beyond the principal corpus of this book in its deconstruction of the link between torture and truth is *not* an Inquisition narrative? Are the Inquisition "histories" I've analyzed here—from the more conservative Magalhães to the heterodox Berman—ultimately inseparable from the logic of the historical events that inspire and haunt them, even as they strive to move away from such reactionary violence? Does the problem have to do with the structure of historical allegory itself, with the stubborn referentiality of the Inquisition? How does Saramago's novel allow us to read this corpus from another angle? Does the notion of an ethics of the event in

Saramago point to unexplored surprises in the other works we've read, or does it make evident that what dominates the phenomenon of Inquisition narratives is nothing more than a reproduction of the violence that makes it possible in the first place?

I want to propose, as a mode of conclusion, an ethics of reading as witnessing that, in its departure from the logic of proof, abandons Inquisitional logic in favor of something more expansive, but also more dangerous. If, at its worst, literary criticism, too, obeys a logic of proof, in which the interrogation of a text results in the narrowing of thought rather than its expansion, can we begin to imagine a critical practice that would hold open multiple possibilities of interpretation? This critical practice would bring us closer to what we now understand literature to be. Literature, or the literary moment in aesthetic discourses, is now to be defined as the device for recording and producing undecidabilities, as well as the writing practice that allows readers to formulate ethical responses to states of affairs found not only in literary works, but in the world at large. Perhaps the only way to begin the anti-inquisitorial inquisitions that this kind of literature requires is to face the void of the impossible that stands at the heart of every creative act as well as its interpretation. If we read the failure of literary discourse in Saramago as a success of sorts, perhaps the work of theory can accompany the task of the literary in its pursuit of new names for such a failure. Just as thinking the event together with the machine remains, according to Derrida in "Typewriter Ribbon," a "monstrosity . . . an impossible event" and "therefore the only possible event" (74), we might understand the contribution of literature—of theory—to debates on torture as supplementary, that—by "seeing" and "saying"—bear witness to the impossible event of truth that stands at the heart of the scene of interrogation.

Notes

PREFACE

1. I first drafted this paragraph in 2009, just after Obama took office. As this book goes to press in 2013, 100 out of the 166 inmates in Guantánamo are on a hunger strike, and the international call to close the prison grows louder every day.

2. Atlantic studies have, until now, mainly focused on issues of power, race, and violence in relation to slavery: while Paul Gilroy's field-defining *The Black Atlantic* (1993) stands as one of the earliest and best-known examples of cultural theory that posits the Atlantic as a site upon which it is possible to read "Blackness" in its various political and cultural forms, Ian Baucom's more recent *Specters of the Atlantic* (2005) places the question of finance capital in the center of the discussion of slavery.

3. The dynamic of conversion as differential inclusion, moreover, can be thought together with the idea of hegemony. As Moreiras convincingly argues, "If *conquisto* means that I take possession of the land in such a way that I enable that which is fallen to participate in its own domination—if *conquisto* is always already imperial according to the Heideggerian determination of *impero*—then differential inclusion is the fundamental device of imperial domination" (Moreiras, "Ten Notes on Primitive Imperial Accumulation," 350).

4. In this book, I oscillate between the terms *marrano, converso, crypto-Jew,* and *New Christian.* While *converso* describes a Jewish convert to Christianity, *marrano* and *New Christian* (*cristão novo* in Portuguese) refer to converts as well as their descendants. A *crypto-Jew* describes the *converso,* marrano, or New Christian who continues to observe Jewish rituals clandestinely (or who is accused of doing so). Following the lead of Ricardo Forster, Jacques Derrida, and Alberto Moreiras, I use *marranismo* to refer to the aporetic, in-between

quality of each of these terms, hoping to move beyond the identitary logic that conditions each of them.

INTRODUCTION

The first chapter epigraph is from United Nations, "Convention Against Torture and Other Cruel, Inhuman or Degrading Treatment or Punishment," December 10, 1984; the second is from Page duBois, *Torture and Truth*, 68. The third epigraph is from Jean-Paul Sartre, preface to *The Question*, by Henri Alleg, 23.

1. Federal Government's Counterterrorism Efforts: Hearing Before the S. Judiciary Subcommittee, 108th Cong. (2004) (statement of Sen. Charles Schumer, Member, S. Judiciary Committee).

2. The number of books and articles whose titles contain both "torture" and "truth" is rather astounding. In addition to Page duBois's *Torture and Truth*, which explores the intimate relationship between violent interrogation and the Western notion of truth beginning in Greek antiquity, Elizabeth Hanson's "Torture and Truth in Renaissance England" and Sophia A. McClennen's "Torture and Truth in Ariel Dorfman's *La muerte y la doncella*" investigate the problem within Elizabethan culture and post-dictatorship Chile, respectively. Mark Danner's *Torture and Truth: America, Abu Ghraib, and the War on Terror* and Jennifer Harbury's *Truth, Torture, and the American Way: The History and Consequences of U.S. Involvement in Torture,* for their part, aim to expose the "truth" about the use of torture by the U.S. government.

3. In the Spanish verb *revelar,* there exists a productive ambiguity between the act of revealing or unconcealing on the one hand, and the idea of "re-velar," to veil or disguise once again. I will return to this idea in my discussion of the secret of the marrano in chapter 1. I thank David E. Johnson for this keen observation.

4. This battle over signification seeped into the realm of the visual as well; indeed, the desire to visually represent these crimes formed a part of the torture itself, challenging Michel Foucault's assertion that torture has ceased to be a public spectacle. That representation—visual representation in particular—is at the very heart of the practice of torture leads to a crucial issue. If, as Elaine Scarry argues, physical pain is unrepresentable, what role can we assign to representation in the seemingly mutually exclusive acts of practicing and resisting torture?

5. Idelber Avelar discusses the problematic status of the notions of "self," "voice," and "civilization," which, he argues, are left unquestioned by Scarry (Avelar, "Five Theses on Torture," 255, 258–60).

6. In the case of the Spanish anarchists (or any other militant movement), we are not speaking of a regime, but a political entity whose authoritative instability similarly calls for the "unmaking" of the enemy in order to assert power. While I will not elaborate on this here, it would be interesting to reflect upon the crucial difference between the use of torture by anarchist rebels and totalitarian regimes. For the purpose of the present discussion, however, the distinction is largely immaterial.

7. This scene dramatizes the link between torture and truth: the forced confession reveals the true location of the target (Ali la Pointe) as the fake wall is

removed to expose the faces of la Pointe and his collaborators. In his analysis of the configuration of terror in *The Battle of Algiers,* Jacques Lezra argues for a double sense of female unveiling in the film (see "Three Women, Three Bombs" in *Wild Materialism*). Revelation, then, is not necessarily all it seems to be.

8. *The Battle of Algiers* has been critiqued on a number of fronts, among them Joan Mellen's argument that the film equates colonial violence with the violence of the Algerian insurgents in "An Interview with Gillo Pontecorvo," *Film Quarterly* 26, no. 1 (1972): 2–10.

CHAPTER 1

The first chapter epigraph is from Ricardo Forster, "La aventura marrana," 155; the second is from Jacques Derrida, *Aporias,* 81.

1. The epigraph for this section is from Jacques Derrida, "Passions: An Oblique Offering," 23–24.

2. As I detail in chapter 3, de Man explains that "what Rousseau *really* wanted is neither the ribbon nor Marion, but the public scene of exposure which he actually gets. . . . The more crime there is, the more theft, lie, slander, and stubborn persistence in each of them, the better. The more there is to expose, the more there is to be ashamed of; the more resistance to exposure, the more satisfying the scene, and, especially, the more satisfying and eloquent the belated revelation, in the later narrative, or the inability to reveal" (*Allegories of Reading,* 285).

3. Derrida engages with this argument in the essay that follows in *Without Alibi,* "Typewriter Ribbon."

4. "It's that if I am a sort of *Marrano* of French Catholic culture, and I also have my Christian body, inherited from SA in a more or less twisted line, *condiebar eius sale,* I am one of those *Marranos* who no longer say they are Jews even in the secret of their own hearts, not so as to be authenticated *Marranos* on both sides of the public frontier, but because they doubt everything, never go to confession or give up enlightenment, whatever the cost, ready to have themselves burned, almost" (Derrida, qtd. in Cixous, 86–87).

5. In a recent essay, Alberto Moreiras postulates the idea of a "marrano register" as a tradition of thought that, since Spinoza, marks a point of resistance against (and within) identitarian thought and imperial domination: "What is the *marrano* register? It is the short name of what we should properly call a *converso-marrano* register. *Converso* references the abandonment of what was previously one's own in order to embrace a social truth, a dominant state of the situation. And marrano is the state of return, or rather the melancholy state where the shadow of the lost object falls upon the subject and splits it or destabilizes it. I am making obvious reference to Spanish and Portuguese Jewish history and its avatars, without question a point of torsion of a history of the practice of freedom that, as such, has never relented in its struggle against the logics of imperial domination" ("Common Political Democracy," 175–76).

6. "There is no ceremony, however public and exposed, which does not revolve around a secret, even if it is the secret of a nonsecret" (Derrida, "Passions," 7).

7. "We testify [*témoignons*] to a secret that is without content, without a content separable from its performative experience, from its performative tracing. (We shall not say from its performative *enunciation* or from its *propositional argumentation;* and we keep in reserve a number of questions about performativity in general)" (Derrida, "Passions," 24).

8. If for Derrida "what is proper to the Jew is to have no property or essence" ("Shibboleth," 35), the figure of the marrano radicalizes this aporetic relation between essentialism and anti-essentialism, between the secret as positive content and the secret as radical singularity. In "Shibboleth," the idea of *partage* in French is read as simultaneously signaling parting, dividing, excluding *and* inclusion, belonging, taking part, pertinence, so that Jewishness (and identity in general) would refer to that which divides as it binds. I will return to this discussion in my reading of circumcision below.

9. The title epigraph for this section is from Forster, "La aventura marrana," 155.

10. Zygmunt Bauman (*Modernity and the Holocaust*, 37), Tamar Garb ("Introduction," 20), and Erin Graff Zivin (*The Wandering Signifier*, 5) all refer to Judaism's paradoxical role as both the source and limit of Christianity.

11. For a discussion of the presence of New Christians in colonial Latin America, see Anita Novinsky (*Cristãos Novos na Bahia*), Judith Laikin Elkin (*Jews of Latin America*), and María Elena Martínez (*Genealogical Fictions*).

12. Yovel contends that "powerful identity passions, serving as carrier to economic and social rivalries, worked to reject the Conversos" (*The Other Within*, 59).

13. For more on this, see Graff Zivin, "Conversiones textuales," 260; and Graff Zivin, *The Wandering Signifier*, 5–7, 119–24.

14. The year 1492 symbolically marks a broader moment in which national unification coincides with (and depends upon) the expulsion and conversion of internal "others" and the conquest of the Americas. In this sense, Inquisition and imperialism are intimately linked in both historical-material terms as well as in structural or philosophical terms. Oscar Cabezas details the Foucaultian notion of *pouvoir-savoir* in the context of the Expulsion in the following way: "El exilio como éxodo forzado, la persecución, el miedo al otro, la tortura, el debilitamiento de las creencias a partir del amedrentamiento, el desmembramiento de grupos sospechosos ante la 'verdad' que custodia las instituciones modernas del poder, conforman la constante moderna de un saber inquisitorial inscrito en las instituciones policiales del poder" ("Edicto de 1492," 101). The relationship between Inquisition and colonialism will be explored further in chapter 2.

15. As I detail in *The Wandering Signifier*, representations of literal and figurative conversions of Jews can be found in a diverse number of texts both within and outside of the Luso-Hispanic literary tradition, among which are William Shakespeare's *The Merchant of Venice* (1600), Justo Sierra O'Reilly's *La hija del judío* (1848), Jorge Isaacs's *María* (1867), Joaquim Maria Machado de Assis's "A cristã nova" (1875), Benito Pérez Galdós's *Gloria* (1877) as well as his *Torquemada* novels (1884, 1886–87, 1889), Victor Hugo's *Torquemada* (1882), George Eliot's *Daniel Deronda* (1876), James Joyce's *Ulysses* (1922), Heitor Carlos Cony's *Pessach: A travessia* (1967), Antonio Gala's *Las cítaras*

colgadas de los árboles (1974), Mario Vargas Llosa's *El hablador* (1987), and Carme Riera's *En el último azul* (1996). See Ragussis, *Figures of Conversion;* and Shapiro, *Shakespeare and the Jews,* for more on the presence of Jewish conversion in the British literary tradition.

16. I will not discuss Portuguese novelist Camilo Castelo Branco's 1866 *O Judeu* here, though I would like to note its existence.

17. The social and political milieu of 1970s PRI-dominated Mexico, the period during which *El Santo Oficio* was written and produced, will be treated in my discussion of the film's allegorical quality in chapter 2.

18. Unless otherwise stated, all citations are taken from the published screenplay, while discussion of visual aspects of the work refer to the cinematographic version of the film.

19. Derrida describes circumcision as a "carnal mark at once endowed with and deprived of singularity" ("Shibboleth," 54).

20. Bensadon argues that "the fact that Luis decides to circumcise himself directly after his encounter with [prostitute] Justa [Mendez] and exclaiming the circumcision as a sacrifice are indicative of the Catholic influences in his interiority" (*Modernity and Crisis,* 73).

21. The act (and the crime) of circumcision is a central trope in Derrida's autobiographical, "confessional" piece, "Circumfession." He also describes the aporetic singularity of circumcision (it happens only once, it is the infinite repetition of a ritual) in "Shibboleth: For Paul Celan" (1–2).

22. Berman's play was first published as *Anatema* in 1983, debuted as *Herejía* in 1984, and was then expanded and published as *En el nombre de Dios* in 1991.

23. References to the work in Spanish are from *En el nombre de Dios,* unless otherwise stated. Descriptions and citations in English are guided by Adam Versényi's translation of *Heresy.*

24. I discuss the interpellative quality of interrogation in chapter 3.

25. In the scene immediately preceding Luisito's name change, Don Luis and Felipe Nuñez discuss his potential as a successor. Out of jealousy, Felipe warns Don Luis that he seems a bit "deshilachado" (Berman, *En el nombre de Dios,* 338) ("frayed" [Berman, *Heresy,* 125]). Don Luis claims to be able to detect a hint of nobility in him, promising that "Ya lo vestiremos como Dios manda" (338) ("We'll dress him up like a little duke soon enough") (125). The idea that nobility (thought at the time to be an essential characteristic, represented through the idea of purity of blood) can be donned like a costume is crucial to the deconstruction of identity in Berman. I will discuss the performative quality of marrano identity in Berman later in this section. Interestingly, it is Luisito's penchant for poetry that has Don Luis most worried: "No me resulte poeta, coño, toque madera" (338) ("he'd better not turn out to be a poet, fuck, knock on wood").

26. Translation based loosely on *Heresy* (143–44).

27. This scene is absent from *Herejía* and only appears in the later version, *En el nombre de Dios.*

28. Severino João Albuquerque argues that, in fact, this widely held belief is an error propagated by Magalhães's own self-publicity ("The Brazilian The-

atre," 112). Albuquerque describes Magalhães's first play as "a supposedly romantic work that follows neoclassical dictates, a 'tragedy' that does not qualify as such, and . . . a 'Brazilian' play set outside the country" (113).

29. For more on Jewish conversion narratives, see Graff Zivin, "Conversiones textuales" and *The Wandering Signifier.*

30. In Santareno, Antônio José's name is spelled António José.

31. I am grateful to Jonathan Freedman for pointing me in the direction of this reading.

32. In his discussion of Plato's allegory of the cave, Samuel Weber alludes to the destabilizing quality of puppetry, arguing that "even today puppets exemplify the aspect of theatricality which has caused it to be regarded with suspicion by a certain humanistic tradition: its heterogeneity" (*Theatricality as Medium,* 6).

33. While not unrelated to de Man's (and before him, Austin's) work on performative language, Butler's analysis of performativity is rooted in visibility and eventness. Samuel Weber's work on theatricality as medium (rather than genre) might help us to understand both de Man's linguistic performative *and* Butler's gender performance as linked to the destabilizing potential of the event.

CHAPTER 2

The first epigraph for this chapter is from Walter Benjamin, *The Origin of German Tragic Drama,* 193; the second is from Paul de Man, *Allegories of Reading,* 205.

1. In addition to the broader Jewish conversion narratives to which I refer in the previous chapter, a subgenre of Inquisition allegories emerges during and in the wake of authoritarian regimes in Latin America and the Iberian Peninsula in the 1960s and 1970s. Brazilian playwright Alfredo Dias Gomes's *O Santo Inquérito* (1966), Spanish playwright Antonio Gala's *Las cítaras colgadas de los árboles* (1974), Spanish playwright and filmmaker Fernando Arrabal's *Inquisición* (1979), Chilean novelist Guillermo Blanco's *Camisa limpia* (1989), and Argentine novelist Marcos Aguinis's *La gesta del marrano* (1991) are the best-known examples.

2. I borrow this idea from Samuel Weber's discussion of Benjaminian allegory in *Theatricality as Medium,* in which he argues that "the key to an understanding of [*Origin of German Tragic Drama*] lies not only in an examination of the question of allegory, nor even in the distinction between the 'genres' of tragedy and *Trauerspiel* . . . , but rather in the relation between the two: between the significance of the *Trauerspiel,* on the one hand, and that of allegory, on the other. Such reflection reveals that the *Trauerspiel* is as little a traditional aesthetic *genre* as allegory a device of rhetorical or aesthetical style. Allegory, as Benjamin approaches it, consists above all in a distinctive *mode of signification*" (162).

3. Elsewhere, Derrida addresses the question of allegory more directly as part of his reflection on blindness. He describes allegory as "this strange self-portrait of drawing given over to the speech and gaze of the other" ("Memoirs of the Blind," 3). While I do not have time to discuss here the interplay of orality,

visuality, writing, and drawing in this characteristically dense quotation, I do want to underscore the idea of allegory as a discourse of the self "given over to" the other. The idea of that which is "given over to" the other implies at once a sacrifice, a surrender, an exposure, but also (and perhaps most significantly) that element of identity and its representation which is always already impossible because it is "of the *blind*" and "*of* the blind" ("Memoirs of the Blind," 2).

4. Cohen's neologism suggests "the shifting mechanics of a certain technology of inscription implied," gesturing toward "a conception of (dis)inscription and mnemotechnics which, however banal, might lay claim to a spectral 'materiality'" (*Ideology and Inscription*, 8). In *Hitchcock's Cryptonomies*, Cohen once again links the allegorical to the spectral through the idea of allography, arguing that "the allographic may be thought to produce the figure of a spectral event" (280).

5. Among the narrative works that allegorize Portugal under dictatorship are José Vaz's *A fábula dos feijões cinzentos* (2000), José Saramago's *Ensaio sobre a ceguera* (1995), and Lídia Jorge's *O Dia dos Prodígios* (1979).

6. In her essay "The Question of Awakening in Postdictatorship Times," Susana Draper critiques Avelar's reduction of allegory to the narration of a defeat, sustaining that the contrast between "factual truth" and "truth of the defeat," or between testimonial literature and allegorical literature, "runs the risk of establishing an opposition" between historicism and historicity, factual and allegorical, "that the allegorical in Benjamin already tried to question" (90).

7. Ricardo Piglia's *Respiración artificial* (1980), written during the Argentine *guerra sucia,* serves as a well-known example of this dynamic within the context of the Southern Cone dictatorships. The novel, which investigates the disappearance of Marcelo Maggi by his nephew Renzi, begins with the question, "¿Hay una historia?", raising the issue of the relationship between narrative and experience. The fact that this question can be translated alternatively as "Is there a story?", "Is there a history?", "Is there one story?" or "Is there one history?", as Patrick Dove has made clear (*Catastrophe of Modernity,* 225), suggests that we cannot read Piglia's novel as "about" the disappeared in the context of the Dirty Wars any more than we can read it as "about" the nineteenth century. In the same way, Inquisition narratives that surface in response to non-democratic regimes (Francoist Spain, PRI-dominated Mexico, dictatorship/post-dictatorship Brazil and Portugal) are not merely telling a (decodable) story of the present through the (coded) story of the past. There is instead an unsettling tension *between* these moments and, more precisely, in the impossibility of reading them as disparate. Piglia's question gestures toward an alternate notion of history, a nonlinear version in which the past erupts into the present (and vice versa).

8. Joel Fineman describes "a specifically allegorical desire, a desire for allegory, that is implicit in the idea of structure itself and explicit in criticism that directs itself towards the structurality of literature" ("Structure of Allegorical Desire," 26).

9. Although, as Jenckes reminds us, de Man distinguishes between "temporality," which "denotes a passive unfolding," and "history," which "introduces the possibility of interrupting such unfolding" (Jenckes, *Reading Borges After Benjamin,* xii).

10. The epigraph for this section is from Samuel Weber, *Theatricality as Medium*, 174.

11. "1958: Arthur Miller cleared of contempt." http://news.bbc.co.uk/onthisday/hi/dates/stories/august/7/newsid_2946000/2946420.stm.

12. For Derrida, the specter of the past arrives as if from the future: "what comes before me, before any present, thus before any past present, but also what, for that very reason, comes from the future or as future: as the very coming of the event" (*Specters of Marx*, 33). Responding to the title of the colloquium for which he prepared these lectures ("Whither Marxism?"), Derrida states: "The question is indeed 'whither?' Not only whence comes the ghost but first of all is it going to come back? Is it not already beginning to arrive and where is it going? What of the future? The future can only be for ghosts. And the past" (45).

13. In both scenes, it turns out to be the epidemic that has caused both groups of indigenous and mestizo peasants to seek asylum. But the origin of the epidemic is itself a mystery that has been blamed on the conversos: Luis and Baltasar, in an early scene, stumble upon two monks who warn them "Hay epidemia: dicen que los judíos están envenenando los pozos" (19) ("There's an epidemic: they say that the Jews are poisoning the wells").

14. For more on literary and photopoetic responses to Tlatelolco, see Ryan Long's *Fictions of Totality* (especially chapter 3), chapter 5 of Gareth Williams's *The Mexican Exception*, and Samuel Steinberg's "Re-cinema: Hauntology of 1968" and "'Tlatelolco me bautizó': Literary Renewal and the Neoliberal Transition."

15. The translations of Berman are my own: the scenes discussed here do not appear in the earlier version of the play, *Herejía*.

16. I introduce Weber's idea of theatricality as medium in relation to *marranismo* in chapter 1.

CHAPTER 3

The epigraph for this chapter is from Slavoj Žižek, *The Sublime Object of Ideology*, 178.

1. The first epigraph for this section is from Michel Foucault, *Discipline and Punish*, 5; the second is from Paul de Man, *Allegories of Reading*, 280.

2. The example of Albert Camus's *The Fall*—which, as fiction, does not technically pertain to the genre of autobiography—mimics the genre by occupying the first-person singular throughout the entire text. Despite the fact that the entire novella is, in fact, a conversation, the interlocutor never speaks but is merely insinuated, included in minor allusions within the narrator's speech, and instead serves only as a springboard for the confessional discourse of the narrative subject. In this sense, confession is shown to be nearly as oppressive as interrogative discourse, but from the other side: while the confessional "I" dominates the text in the former, the interrogated—also ultimately confessional—"I" is dominated in the latter.

3. Derrida, too, glosses Saint Augustine's and Rousseau's *Confessions* in "Typewriter Ribbon."

4. As I discuss in chapter 1, Derrida defines the "universal Marrano" as "anyone who remains faithful to a secret that he has not chosen, in the very place where he lives, in the home of the inhabitant or of the occupant, in the home of the first or of the second arrivant, in the very place where he stays without saying no but without identifying himself as belonging to" (*Aporias*, 81).

5. António José Saraiva explains that under the Portuguese Inquisition, once arrested "a person was presumed to be guilty . . . there could be no question of innocence. . . . The goal of the Inquisitors was to elicit a confession—a goal so pious it justified every means" (*The Marrano Factory*, 45).

6. The first epigraph for this section is from Rainer Maria Rilke, quoted in de Man, *Allegories of Reading*, 29; the second is from Franz Kafka, *The Trial*, 29.

7. Indeed, K. is never officially interrogated by the court, a fact that torments him so much that he delivers his own confession-like monologue at the courthouse without ever having been questioned, which turns out to cost him the interrogation that he so desires: "'I just wanted to draw your attention to the fact,' said the examining magistrate, 'that you have today deprived yourself—although you can't yet have realized it—of the advantage that an interrogation offers to the arrested man in each case'" (Kafka, *The Trial*, 52–53).

8. Part of the oversimplification of K's innocence lies in the difficult translation from the German *Böses* to "wrong" in English. The original German betrays a relativity to the declared innocence in "without having done anything wrong," because *Böses* carries with it the allusion to the biblical fall as well as to Nietzsche's idea of morality in *Jenseits von Gut und Böse* (Beyond Good and Evil). Thus, the fact that Josef K. has done nothing truly evil does not exempt him from guilt. (See "Translator's Preface," xix.)

9. This is revisited later in the novel, when the narrator states that "for once the court was going to run into a defendant who knew how to stand up for his rights" (Kafka, *The Trial*, 126). Again, the emphasis is not so much on his innocence but rather on the question of justice.

10. In the film version, it is the lawyer (played by Orson Welles) who relates the parable.

11. Žižek insists that it is, counterintuitively, the residue of failure of interpellation-subjectivation that constitutes the subject as a subject-for-the-Law: "this 'internalization' [of State Apparatuses], by structural necessity, never fully succeeds . . . there is always a residue, a leftover, a stain of traumatic irrationality and senselessness sticking to it, and that *this leftover, far from hindering the full submission of the subject to the ideological command, is the very condition of it*: it is precisely this non-integrated surplus of senseless traumatism which confers on the Law its unconditional authority" (*Sublime Object*, 43).

12. I refer here to the version of the opening interrogation scene as depicted in *Herejía*, the earlier version of *En el nombre de Dios*.

13. I connect the idea of the secret name with the phenomenon of *marranismo* in chapter 1.

14. Sontag details the relationship between pornography and torture in "Regarding the Torture of Others."

15. The idea of the aestheticization of violence as ethical might seem counterintuitive, though I believe it is what Alberto Moreiras refers to in a recent essay

on the Mexican thriller as an ethico-political genre: "Every murder is primarily an ethical breach, an ethical fault. Otherwise it would not be murder. Every murder is a relation to the other, and it is essentially a relation to the other. There is no murder, and there can be no murder, if the 'ethical predication based upon recognition of the other [is] purely and simply abandoned.' There will only be political adjudications of murder. Murder radically suspends the ethical imperative of the radical priority of the other, and it is therefore a negative relation to the other. But the inversion, the negation of a relation does not destroy the relation" (Moreiras, "Infrapolitics and the Thriller," 169). By aesthetically codifying the ethical breach, the work of art dwells within the space of ethics, albeit negatively, and by investigating the scene of the crime, it becomes, in addition to ethical, a political act.

CHAPTER 4

1. The first epigraph for this section is from Jacques Derrida, "History of the Lie," 52; the second is from José Saramago, *Seeing*, 49.

2. There is one mention of "Portugal" in the presidential address to the nation (Saramago, *Ensaio sobre a Lucidez*, 82).

3. Derrida refers to the "radical experience of the *perhaps*" as an ambivalent articulation of the political that simultaneously includes an affirmation and "an experience of the impossible" (*Specters of Marx*, 42).

4. The modernity of the polygraph is debunked here: just as torture focuses on the body as the site of truth (Page duBois explains that it is for this reason that the "truth" of the master must be elicited from the slave, who is understood to behave as a body, rather than the free man, who is seen to act from the mind), the polygraph relies on the overcoming of the mind by the body.

5. Originally a lecture delivered at the UC Davis Center for Humanities in 1998.

Bibliography

Acevedo-Muñoz, Ernesto R. "Horror of Allegory: The Others and Its Context." In *Contemporary Spanish Cinema and Genre*, ed. Jay Beck and Vicente Rodríguez Ortega, 202–18. Manchester, Eng.: Manchester University Press, 2008.

Aguinis, Marcos. *La gesta del marrano*. 1991. Reprint, Buenos Aires: Planeta, 2003.

Albuquerque, Severino João. "The Brazilian Theatre up to 1900." In *Cambridge History of Latin American Literature*, ed. Roberto González Echevarría and Enrique Pupo Walker, 3:105–25. New York: Cambridge University Press, 1996.

Althusser, Louis. "Ideology and Ideological State Apparatuses (Notes Towards an Investigation)." In *Lenin and Philosophy and Other Essays*, trans. Ben Brewster, 127–86. New York: Monthly Review, 1969.

Arrabal, Fernando. *Inquisición*. 1979. Prologue by Angel Bérenguer. Reprint, Granada, Spain: Editorial Don Quijote, 1982.

Avelar, Idelber. "Five Theses on Torture." *Journal of Latin American Cultural Studies* 10, no. 3 (December 2001): 253–71.

———. *The Untimely Present: Postdictatorial Latin American Fiction and the Task of Mourning*. Durham, N.C.: Duke University Press, 1999.

Azulay, Jom Tob. *O Judeu*. Videocassette. Directed by Jom Tob Azulay. 1996. New York: First Run Features, 1996.

Badiou, Alain. *Ethics: An Essay on the Understanding of Evil*. Trans. Peter Hallward. London: Verso, 2002.

Basterra, Gabriela. *Seductions of Fate: Tragic Subjectivity, Ethics, Politics*. London: Palgrave Macmillan, 2004.

Baucom, Ian. *Specters of the Atlantic: Finance Capital, Slavery, and the Philosophy of History*. Durham, N.C.: Duke University Press, 2005.

Bauman, Zygmunt. "Allosemitism: Premodern, Modern, Postmodern." In *Modernity, Culture and "the Jew,"* ed. Bryan Cheyette and Laura Marcus, 188–96. Stanford, Calif.: Stanford University Press, 1998.

———. *Modernity and the Holocaust.* Ithaca, N.Y.: Cornell University Press, 1991.

Benjamin, Walter. *The Origin of German Tragic Drama.* Intro. George Steiner, trans. John Osborne. London: Verso, 2003.

Bensadon, Deborah. *Modernity and Crisis: The Writing of "the Jew" in Trans-Atlantic Literature.* Ph.D. diss., University of Pittsburgh, 2012.

Berman, Sabina. *El bigote.* 1977. In *Puro teatro* (by Berman), 403–14. Mexico D.F.: Fondo de Cultura Económica, 2004.

———. *En el nombre de Dios.* 1991. In *Puro teatro* (by Berman), 329–82. Mexico D.F.: Fondo de Cultura Económica, 2004.

———. *Entre Villa y una mujer desnuda.* 1992. In *Puro teatro* (by Berman), 157–210. Mexico D.F.: Fondo de Cultura Económica, 2004.

———. *Herejía.* 1983. (Orig. titled *Anatema.*) In *Teatro de Sabina Berman,* 147–211. Mexico City: Editores Mexicanos Unidos, 1985.

———. *Heresy.* In *The Theater of Sabina Berman: "The Agony of Ecstasy" and Other Plays* (by Berman), trans. Adam Versényi, 118–63. Carbondale: Southern Illinois University Press, 2003.

Bhabha, Homi. "Of Mimicry and Man: The Ambivalence of Colonial Discourse." *October* 28 (1984): 125–33.

Bigsby, Christopher. Introduction to *The Crucible.* Edited by Arthur Miller. New York: Penguin Books, 2003.

Blanco, Guillermo. *Camisa limpia.* 1989. Santiago, Chile: LOM Ediciones/Universidad ARCIS, 2000.

Brecher, Bob. *Torture and the Ticking Bomb.* London: Wiley-Blackwell, 2007.

Brooks, Peter. *Troubling Confessions: Speaking Guilt in Law and Literature.* Chicago: University of Chicago Press, 2000.

Butler, Judith. *Gender Trouble: Feminism and the Subversion of Identity.* London: Routledge, 1990.

———. *The Psychic Life of Power: Theories in Subjection.* Stanford, Calif.: Stanford University Press, 1997.

Cabezas Villalobos, Oscar. "Edicto de 1492: El registro marrano entre la errancia, la identidad y el exilio." In *Exilio e identidad en el mundo hispánico: reflexiones y representaciones,* ed. Laura López Fernández and Beatriz Caballero Rodríguez, 100–123. Madrid: Biblioteca Virtual Miguel de Cervantes, 2012. http://www.cervantesvirtual.com/obra/exilio-e-identidad-en-el-mundo-hispanico-reflexiones-y-representaciones.

Camus, Albert. *The Fall.* Trans. Justin O'Brien. New York: Vintage Books, 1956.

Castelo Branco, Camilo. *O Judeu.* 1866. In *Obras Completas.* Vol. 5. Porto: Lello & Irmão, 1986.

Cixous, Hèléne. *Portrait of Jacques Derrida as a Young Jewish Saint.* New York: Columbia University Press, 2004.

Coetzee, J. M. "Confession and Double Thoughts: Tolstoy, Rousseau, Dostoevsky." 1985. In *Doubling the Point: Essays and Interviews,* ed. David Attwell, 241–296. Cambridge, Mass.: Harvard University Press, 1992.

Cohen, Tom. *Hitchcock's Cryptonomies*. Volume 1: *Secret Agents*. Minneapolis: University of Minnesota Press, 2005.

―――. *Ideology and Inscription: "Cultural Studies" After Benjamin, de Man, and Bakhtin (Literature, Culture, Theory)*. Cambridge, Eng.: Cambridge University Press, 1998.

Cony, Heitor Carlos. *Pessach: A travessia*. Rio de Janeiro: Editôra Civilização, 1967.

Critchley, Simon. Introduction to *The Cambridge Companion to Levinas*, ed. Simon Critchley and Robert Bernasconi, 1–32. Cambridge, Eng.: Cambridge University Press, 2002.

Crowdus, Gary. Interview with Saadi Yacef. "Terrorism and Torture in *The Battle of Algiers*." *Cineaste* 29, no. 3 (Summer 2004): 30–37.

Danner, Mark. *Torture and Truth: America, Abu Ghraib, and the War on Terror*. New York: New York Review Books, 2004.

de Man, Paul. "Aesthetic Formalization: Kleist's *Über das Marionettentheater*." In *The Rhetoric of Romanticism*, 263–90. New York: Columbia University Press, 1984.

―――. *Allegories of Reading*. New Haven, Conn.: Yale University Press, 1979.

Derrida, Jacques. *Aporias*. Trans. Thomas Dutoit. Stanford, Calif.: Stanford University Press, 1993.

―――. "Before the Law." In *Acts of Literature*, ed. Derek Attridge, 181–220. New York: Routledge, 1992.

―――. "Circumfession." Trans. Geoffrey Bennington. In *Jacques Derrida*, by Geoffrey Bennington and Jacques Derrida, 3–315. Chicago: University of Chicago Press, 1993.

―――. "History of the Lie: Prolegomena." In *Without Alibi*, ed. and trans. Peggy Kamuf, 28–70. Stanford, Calif.: Stanford University Press, 2002.

―――. *Memoirs of the Blind: The Self-Portrait and Other Ruins*. Trans. Pascale-Anne Brault and Michael Naas. Chicago: University of Chicago Press, 1993.

―――. "Passions: 'An Oblique Offering.'" In *On the Name*, ed. Thomas Dutoit, trans. David Wood, John P. Leavey Jr., and Ian McLeod, 3–31. Stanford: Stanford University Press, 1995.

―――. "Shibboleth: For Paul Celan." In *Sovereignties in Question: The Poetics of Paul Celan*, ed. Thomas Dutoit and Outi Pasanen, 1–64. New York: Fordham University Press, 2005.

―――. *Specters of Marx: The State of Debt, the Work of Mourning, and the New International*. Trans. Peggy Kamuf. New York: Routledge, 1994.

―――. "Typewriter Ribbon: Limited Ink (2)." In *Without Alibi*, ed. and trans. Peggy Kamuf, 71–160. Stanford, Calif.: Stanford University Press, 2002.

Derrida, Jacques, and Bernard Stiegler. *Echographies of Television*. Trans. Jennifer Bajorek. Cambridge, Mass.: Polity, 2002.

Dias Gomes, Alfredo de Freitas. *O Santo Inquérito*. Rio de Janeiro: Editôra Civilização Brasileira, 1966.

Dolar, Mladen. "Beyond Interpellation." *Qui Parle* 6, no. 2 (1993): 75–96.

Dove, Patrick. *The Catastrophe of Modernity: Tragedy and the Nation in Latin American Literature*. Lewisburg, Pa.: Bucknell University Press, 2004.

Draper, Susana. "The Question of Awakening in Postdictatorship Times." *Discourse* 32, no. 1 (2010): 87–116.

duBois, Page. *Torture and Truth*. New York: Routledge, 1991.

Eliot, George. *Daniel Deronda*. 1876. New York: Harper, 1961.

Elkin, Judith Laikin. *The Jews of Latin America*. New York: Holmes and Meier, 1998.

Evans, Peter William. "El espíritu de la colmena: The Monster, the Place of the Father, and Growing Up in the Dictatorship." *Vida Hispánica* 31, no. 3 (1982): 13–17.

Fineman, Joel. "The Structure of Allegorical Desire." In *Allegory and Representation*, ed. Stephen J. Greenblatt, 26–60. Baltimore: Johns Hopkins University Press, 1981.

Forster, Ricardo. "La aventura marrana en la constitución del sujeto moderno: Claves para comprender la entrada del judaismo en la época de la secularización." In *Mesianismo, Nihilismo y Redención: De Abraham a Spinoza, de Marx a Benjamin*, ed. Ricardo Forster and Diego Tatián, 143–203. Buenos Aires: Altamira, 2005.

Foucault, Michel. *Discipline and Punish*. Trans. Alan Sheridan. New York: Random House, 1995.

Gala, Antonio. *Las cítaras colgadas de los árboles*. 1974. Reprint, Madrid: Preyson, 1983.

Garb, Tamar. "Introduction: Modernity, Identity, Textuality." In *The Jew in the Text: Modernity and the Construction of Identity*, ed. Linda Nochlin and Tamar Garb, 20–30. London: Thames and Hudson, 1995.

Gilroy, Paul. *The Black Atlantic: Modernity and Double Consciousness*. Cambridge, Mass.: Harvard University Press, 1993.

Gonçalves de Magalhães, Domingos José. *O poeta e a inquisição. Drama em 5 atos*. 1838. Reprint, Rio de Janeiro: Serviço Nacional de Teatro, Ministério da Educação e Cultura, 1972.

Graff Zivin, Erin. "Conversiones textuales, inquisiciones transatlánticas: La figura de la cristiana nueva en Dias Gomes y Antonio Gala." *Journal of Spanish Cultural Studies* 6, no. 3 (2005): 259–69.

———. *The Wandering Signifier: Rhetoric of Jewishness in the Latin American Imaginary*. Durham, N.C.: Duke University Press, 2008.

Hanson, Elizabeth. "Torture and Truth in Renaissance England." *Representations* 34 (1991): 53–84.

Harbury, Jennifer. *Truth, Torture, and the American Way: The History and Consequences of U.S. Involvement in Torture*. Boston: Beacon, 2005.

Hersh, Seymour M. "Torture at Abu Ghraib." *New Yorker Magazine*, May 10, 2004. http://www.newyorker.com/archive/2004/05/10/040510fa_fact.

Hugo, Victor. *Torquemada*. 1882. Reprint, Lanham, Md.: University Press of America, 1989.

Hytner, Nicholas. *The Crucible*. DVD. Directed by Nicholas Hytner. Los Angeles: 20th Century Fox, 1996.

Isaacs, Jorge. *María*. 1867. Reprint, Caracas: Biblioteca Ayacucho, 1978.

Jameson, Fredric. "World Literature in an Age of Multinational Capitalism." In *The Current in Criticism: Essays on the Present and Future of Literary*

Theory, ed. Clayton Koelb and Virgil Lokke, 139–58. West Lafayette, Ind.: Purdue University Press, 1986.

Jay, Martin. *Downcast Eyes: The Denigration of Vision in Twentieth-Century French Thought.* Berkeley: University of California Press, 1994.

Jenckes, Kate. *Reading Borges After Benjamin: Allegory, Afterlife, and the Writing of History.* Albany: SUNY Press, 2007.

Jorge, Lídia. *O Dia dos Prodígios.* Lisbon: Publicações Europa-América, 1979.

Joyce, James. *Ulysses.* 1922. Reprint, New York: Random House, 1981.

Kafka, Franz. *The Castle.* 1926. Trans. Mark Harman. Reprint, New York: Schocken Books, 1998.

———. *The Trial.* 1925. Trans. Breon Mitchell. Reprint, New York: Schocken Books, 1999.

———. *The Trial.* DVD. Directed by Orson Welles. New York: Astor Pictures Corporation, 1962.

Kamuf, Peggy. "Introduction: Event of Resistance." In Jacques Derrida, *Without Alibi,* ed. and trans. Peggy Kamuf, 1–27. Stanford: Stanford University Press, 2002.

Kennedy, Rory. *Ghosts of Abu Ghraib.* DVD. Directed by Rory Kennedy. Santa Monica, Calif.: HBO Films, 2007.

Kinder, Marsha. *Blood Cinema: The Reconstruction of National Identity in Spain.* Berkeley: University of California Press, 1993.

Labanyi, Jo. "Memory and Modernity in Democratic Spain: The Difficulty of Coming to Terms with the Spanish Civil War." *Poetics Today* 28, no. 1 (2007): 89–116.

Legras, Horacio. *Literature and Subjection: The Economy of Writing and Marginality in Latin America.* Pittsburgh, Pa.: University of Pittsburgh Press, 2008.

Leung, Rebecca. "Abuse of Iraqi POWs by GIs Probed." *60 Minutes II.* April 28, 2004. http://www.cbsnews.com/2100-500164_162-614063.html.

Levin, Michael. "The Case for Torture." *Newsweek,* June 7, 1982, 7.

Levinas, Emmanuel. *Basic Philosophical Writings.* Ed. Adriaan T. Peperzak, Simon Critchley, and Robert Bernasconi. Bloomington: Indiana University Press, 1996.

———. *Otherwise than Being, or Beyond Essence.* Trans. Alphonso Lingis. 1974. Reprint, Pittsburgh, Pa.: Duquesne University Press, 1998.

———. "Philosophy and the Idea of the Infinite." Trans. Alphonso Lingis. In *To the Other,* ed. Adriaan Peperzak, 88–119. West Lafayette, Ind.: Purdue University Press, 1993.

Lezra, Jacques. *Wild Materialism: The Ethic of Terror and the Modern Republic.* New York: Fordham University Press, 2010.

Long, Ryan F. *Fictions of Totality: The Mexican Novel, 1968, and the National-Popular State.* West Lafayette, Ind.: Purdue University Press, 2008.

Machado de Assis, Joaquim Maria. "A Cristã Nova." 1875. In *Obra completa,* ed. Afrânio Coutinho, 3:110–215. Rio de Janeiro: J. Aguilar, 1962–71.

Martínez, María Elena. *Genealogical Fictions: Limpieza de Sangre, Religion, and Gender in Colonial Mexico.* Stanford, Calif.: Stanford University Press, 2008.

Martí-Olivella, Jaume. "Regendering Spain's Political Bodies: Nationality and Gender in the Films of Pilar Miró and Arantxa Lazcano." In *Refiguring Spain: Cinema/Media/Representation,* ed. Marsha Kinder, 215–38. Durham, N.C.: Duke University Press, 2007.

McClennen, Sophia A. "Torture and Truth in Ariel Dorfman's *La muerte y la doncella.*" *Revista Hispánica Moderna* 62, no. 2 (2009): 179–195.

Mellen, Joan. Interview with Gillo Pontecorvo. *Film Quarterly* 26, no. 1 (1972): 2–10.

Miller, Arthur. *The Crucible.* 1953. Reprint, New York: Penguin Books, 2003.

Moreiras, Alberto. "Common Political Democracy: The Marrano Register." In *Impasses of the Post-Global: Theory in the Era of Climate Change,* vol. 2, ed. Henry Sussman, 175–93. Ann Arbor, Mich.: Open Humanities Press.

———. *The Exhaustion of Difference: The Politics of Latin American Cultural Studies.* Durham, N.C.: Duke University Press, 2001.

———. "Infrapolitics and the Thriller: A Prolegomenon to Every Possible Form of Antimoralist Literary Criticism. On Héctor Aguilar Camín's *La guerra de Galio* and *Morir en el golfo.*" In *The Ethics of Latin American Literary Criticism: Reading Otherwise,* ed. Erin Graff Zivin, 147–79. New York: Palgrave Macmillan, 2007.

———. "Spanish Nation Formation: An Introduction." *Journal of Spanish Cultural Studies* 2, no. 1 (2001): 5–11.

———. "Ten Notes on Primitive Imperial Accumulation: Ginés de Sepúlveda, Las Casas, Fernández de Oviedo." *Interventions* 2, no. 3 (2000): 343–63.

———. *Tercer Espacio: Literatura y duelo en América Latina.* Santiago, Chile: LOM Ediciones / Universidad ARCIS, 1995.

"1958: Arthur Miller Cleared of Contempt." *BBC News.* http://news.bbc.co.uk/onthisday/hi/dates/stories/august/7/newsid_2946000/2946420.stm.

Novinsky, Anita. *Cristãos Novos na Bahia.* São Paulo, Brazil: Universidade de São Paulo & Editora Perspectiva, 1970.

Pérez Galdós, Benito. *Gloria.* 1877. Reprint, Madrid: Libreria y Casa Editorial Hernando, 1963.

———. *Las novelas de Torquemada: Torquemada en la hoguera; Torquemada en la cruz; Torquemada en el purgatorio; Torquemada y San Pedro.* 1893–95. 2nd ed. Reprint, Madrid: Alianza Editorial, 1970.

Piglia, Ricardo. *Respiración artificial.* 1980. Reprint, Buenos Aires: Seix Barral, Biblioteca Breve, 2000.

Pontecorvo, Gillo. *The Battle of Algiers.* DVD. Directed by Gillo Pontecorvo. Morton Grove, Ill.: Criterion, 1967.

Ragussis, Michael. *Figures of Conversion: "The Jewish Question" & English National Identity.* Durham, N.C.: Duke University Press, 1995.

Riera, Carme. *En el último azul.* Madrid: Alfaguara, 1996.

Ripstein, Arturo. *El Santo Oficio.* Videocassette. Directed by Arturo Ripstein. Lima: Conacine, 1974.

Ripstein, Arturo, and José Emilio Pacheco. *El Santo Oficio.* Culiacán, Sinaloa: Universidad Autónoma de Sinaloa, 1980.

Riva Palacio, Vicente. *El Libro Rojo.* México: Pola, 1871.

Rousseau, Jean-Jacques. *The Confessions.* 1781. Trans. J. M. Cohen. Reprint, New York: Penguin Books, 1953.

Santareno, Bernardo. *O Crime da Aldeia Velha*. Lisbon: Edições Atica, 1959.
———. *O Judeu: narrativa dramática em trés actos*. Lisbon: Edições Atica, 1966.
Saraiva, José António. *The Marrano Factory: The Portuguese Inquisition and Its New Christians 1536–1765*. Trans. H. P. Salomon and I. S. D. Sassoon. Reprint, Leiden: Brill, 2001.
Saramago, Jose. *Blindness*. Trans. Juan Sager. Orlando: Harcourt Books, 1997.
———. *Ensaio sobre a Ceguera*. Lisbon: Editorial Caminho, 1995.
———. *Ensaio sobre a Lucidez*. Lisbon: Editorial Caminho, 2004.
———. *Seeing*. Trans. Margaret Jull Costa. Orlando: Harcourt Books, 2006.
Sartre, Jean-Paul. Preface to *The Question*, ed. Henri Alleg, trans. John Calder, 13–36. New York: George Braziller, 1958.
Scarry, Elaine. *The Body in Pain. The Making and Unmaking of the World*. New York: Oxford University Press, 1985.
Shakespeare, William. *The Merchant of Venice*. 1598. Reprint, Cambridge, Eng.: Cambridge University Press, 2003.
Shapiro, James. *Shakespeare and the Jews*. New York: Columbia University Press, 1996.
Sierra O'Reilly, Justo. *La hija del judío*. 1848. Ed. Antonio Castro Leal. Reprint, 2 vols. Mexico City: Editorial Porrúa, S.A., 1959.
Smith, Paul Julian. *The Theatre of García Lorca: Text, Performance, Psychoanalysis*. Cambridge, Eng.: Cambridge University Press, 1998.
Sommer, Doris. *Foundational Fictions: The National Romances of Latin America*. Berkeley: University of California Press, 1991.
Sontag, Susan. "Regarding the Torture of Others." *The New York Times Magazine*, May 23, 2004, 24–41.
Steinberg, Samuel. "Re-cinema: Hauntology of 1968." *Discourse* 33, no. 1 (2011): 3–26.
———. "'Tlatelolco me bautizó': Literary Renewal and the Neoliberal Transition." *Mexican Studies/Estudios Mexicanos* 28, no. 2 (2012): 265–86.
United Nations. "Convention Against Torture and Other Cruel, Inhuman or Degrading Treatment or Punishment." December 10, 1984.
U.S. Congress. Senate. Federal Government's Counterterrorism Efforts: Hearing before the Judiciary Subcommittee (Statement of Charles Schumer, Senator, 108th Congress. 2004).
Vargas Llosa, Mario. *El hablador*. Barcelona: Editorial Seix Barral, 1987.
Vaz, José. *A fábula dos feijões cinzentos*. Lisbon: Editora Campo das Letras, 2000.
von Kleist, Heinrich. "On the Marionette Theater." 1810. *Southern Cross Review* 9 (2000). http://southerncrossreview.org/9/kleist.htm.
Weber, Samuel. *Theatricality as Medium*. New York: Fordham University Press, 2004.
Williams, Gareth. *The Mexican Exception: Sovereignty, Police, and Democracy*. New York: Palgrave Macmillan, 2011.
Yovel, Yirmiyahu. *The Other Within: The Marranos: Split Identity and Emerging Modernity*. Princeton, N.J.: Princeton University Press, 2009.
Žižek, Slavoj. *Interrogating the Real: Selected Writings*. New York: Continuum, 2005.
———. *The Sublime Object of Ideology*. London: Verso, 1989.

Index